Anonymous

Translation of the Mortgage Law

for Cuba, Puerto Rico, and the Phillippines - 1893

Anonymous

Translation of the Mortgage Law
for Cuba, Puerto Rico, and the Phillippines - 1893

ISBN/EAN: 9783337378523

Printed in Europe, USA, Canada, Australia, Japan

Cover: Foto ©Andreas Hilbeck / pixelio.de

More available books at **www.hansebooks.com**

or

THE MORTGAGE LAW

for

CUBA, PUERTO RICO, AND THE PHILIPPINES.

(1893.)

WAR DEPARTMENT,
1899.

WASHINGTON:
GOVERNMENT PRINTING OFFICE.
1899.

MORTGAGE LAW

FOR

CUBA, PUERTO RICO AND THE PHILIPPINES.

TO THE CORTES

The mortgage law, which has been in force in the Peninsula for the past thirty years, was applied to the Antilles, with such changes as were indispensable for its adaptation to those islands, on May 1, 1880, and to the Philippines on December 1, 1889, reforming the laws regarding real property in those countries, and consequently giving a new impetus to land securities. Although this work is not without its imperfections, being human, the mortgage law must be looked upon as one of our most important legal works, and all that is fundamental therein, and even that which appears of less value, should be religiously respected as long as the results of experience and the necessity of reconciling it with the other legal measures in force permit its observance. This has been the rule adhered to by the Government in the preparation of the revision herewith submitted to the Cortes.

The Civil Code for the Colonies as well as for the Peninsula, among other special laws, left the mortgage law expressly in force, without eliminating from it, or diverting from itself entirely, provisions which by their nature would have corresponded to the Code had both originated at the same period. It was an inevitable necessity, therefore, to overcome the differences, and in the revision which took place with this object in view, it was concluded that the Code should prevail whenever a question arose, and not only support the structure of the mortgage law, but that said law should be the only one for all ultramarine provinces; and, further, that it should coincide, as far as possible, with the text of the Peninsular law, thus avoiding the confusion and practical difficulties which were noted in the quotations and references by reason of four different sets of numbers for the articles.

The necessity of harmonizing these differences between the law mentioned and the code is not the only motive which animates the government in presenting this plan. Experience and the especial conditions of real property in some of the ultramarine provinces also urgently suggest, and even demand, important amendments, which naturally, however, should retain the cardinal principles of the system.

3

The law having been enacted so that all real property should be recorded in authentic official books, it was at once observed that a considerable portion was not subjected to this beneficent rule, by which it could be freed from usury and its possession guaranteed. The taxes, the schedule of notarial and register's fees, and the complications as well as the requirements of form, made this object of the legislator unattainable. It was necessary to remove these obstacles, so that small properties could enjoy the advantages of credit. Furthermore, the omission of the record of deeds keeps from the registry a considerable portion of land, and as this evil can only be remedied by notices of possession, it is advisable to still further facilitate them, notwithstanding the undesirable features thereof, by permitting their conversion into absolute titles twenty years after their date. These two reforms have already been fully discussed by the Senate, and were approved in 1890, in order to incorporate them in the Peninsular law.

At that time another reform was also considered which had been urgently demanded. The old books of property, which were to be replaced by those created by the mortgage law, contained a multitude of liens and claims which had absolutely expired, but had not been canceled in a definite manner, thus depreciating the value of property without reason.

It was an urgent requisite of credit to declare those books without force as to third persons after a certain period, and it was therefore proposed that all persons who had any interest recorded in the same should transfer them to the new books if they desired the State to force third persons to respect them. By reenforcing this provision in giving greater scope to proceedings for clearing the title, the certificate of a register will indicate the legal status of the realty, thus giving contracts the security which they should enjoy.

But where the voice of experience has been heard with the greatest clamor against the law, demanding immediate relief, is where it refers to the procedure for making mortgage debts effective. Its crushing confusion, the uncertainty of results, and its incalculable cost restrain capital or suggest usurious conditions; sales and resales take the place of loans, with the object of avoiding all proceedings to the prejudice of the landowner; interest is stipulated which triplicates the capital loaned, and perhaps by the employment of other means the debtor is exposed to penal responsibility, converting the sanctity of laws enacted for the punishment of crimes into a vile instrument of avarice against the unfortunate. Distrust causes these means to be employed because the legal procedure does not satisfy the reasonable requisites of contracts, and to uproot these evils, to furnish land with the capital it needs, and to give the lender assurances of speedy and easy recovery of his loans, is the object of the most important reform proposed by the Government, suppressing proceedings which, without positively guaranteeing one's rights, destroy those most sacred. Previous appraisement, uniformity of judicial action in all necessary investigations, suppression of all litigation, only one summons and the immediate sale by auction, are the basis of the new law. We have abolished suits, exemptions, letters requisitorial (exhortos), writs of attachment on the mortgaged property, proceedings in the nature of a demurrer, simultaneous auctions, and a great many other barriers in the path of the credit of realty, which had been placed with the best of intentions, but from which those in good faith were the only victims.

The special conditions existing in the ultramarine provinces have suggested other amendments, especially for the Island of Cuba. The reforms mentioned, equally useful for Puerto Rico and the Philippines, have been proposed in accordance with the crisis which is complained of with regard to the development of their credit on real property, but all of them would be worthless without the enactment of a measure which has been unanimously and most justly demanded, and which will in itself promote credit and prevent the repetition of the statement that in Cuba there as yet exist no mortgage regulations. This measure consists in abolishing the time, which has been indefinitely extended by royal decree of May 6, 1882, during which mortgages as well as other implied liens remain in force; these secret incumbrances, which do not appear in the registry, rendering all contracts involving realty hazardous, although they appear completely unencumbered according to the record. The time which was just and reasonable during a period of transition, and which was allowed in the Peninsula, Puerto Rico, and the Philippines, has already lapsed, while it is still running in Cuba, and has been for the past thirteen years, placing all parties to contracts in a state of uncertainty and causing them to be suspicious. The new law will fix a time for its termination, which will not be extended.

Credit of land requires more. On account of the provisions of articles 73 to 78 of the Cuban mortgage law loans are now reduced to 50 per cent of the value of estates, said articles reserving the other half for the security of subsequent lenders, who may wish to aid the cultivation and production of the soil. These articles place such obstacles and difficulties in the way of such loans, incorrectly called "agricultural loans" (refaccionarios), that, according to all information, the privilege is not made use of in practice, and in point of fact this compensation for the evil suffered by mortgage contract is lacking. To reestablish credit of lands to its fullest extent by the abolition of these articles is to comply with a legitimate demand of Cuban land owners whom it is intended to protect.

The law fills another requisite. To facilitate the acquisition on time payments of machines and other agricultural implements it is necessary that the simple attachment to the soil of an article sold, when the vendor has not yet been fully paid, should not turn it over to the mercy of prior mortgage creditors, inasmuch as subsequent acquisitions of the debtor are not security for the fulfillment of their contracts. The provisions of paragraph 2 of article 112 of the new law correct this fault, which was a great impediment in the way of a perfect and strong reestablishment of Cuban industries.

Two other reforms which are demanded by that island have no appropriate place in the mortgage law, and will, therefore, have to be otherwise disposed of, viz, loans which are secured only by the products and the survey of estates owned by tenants in common. This law, embracing real property only, can not be applied to products when considered apart from the soil itself; agricultural credit can not be considered as embraced by a credit of the land. The survey of estates of tenants in common is in that island a question of as great difficulty in its social aspect as the question of emphyteusis in Galicia, and pertains to the Civil Code and the Code of Procedure, and not to a law which presupposes and requires that the property already is surveyed to give publicity and permanent stability to its legal situation.

An attempt was made some time ago to apply the registry system known by the name of "Acta Torrens" to the Philippines, but the confusion which would attend a radical change of system within four years of the establishment of the present one, and when the last quarterly statistics show that it is becoming customary and generalized, and together with an examination of the former system with regard to the condition of property in the Philippines, the Government has desisted from that intention, which, furthermore, could not be effected without making considerable changes in civil law and without involving the public treasury in hazardous and indefinite responsibilities. Our mortgage law, which already had a large number of precedents in the Archipelago, can be reformed by slight amendments, which, together with the reforms of the provisions regarding the readjustment of royal patrimonies, will pave the way for the advent of the institutions of credit for lands, which is based on a sound mortgage law, and legally recorded deeds, which define and secure all interests in the land.

It would be superfluous to repeat here the benefits which may be expected in Puerto Rico through these reforms. The institution of the registry is running smoothly there, without causing complaints, and now, in giving greater power and clearness to the same system, it is logical to expect that its salutary effects will increase.

To undertake the reforms mentioned, the Government depended on various legal authorizations, but the vote of the Cortes is necessary to put an end to implied mortgages, according to the text of article 3 of the royal decree of May 6, 1882. It appears desirable, therefore, to go beyond the limit which those authorizations seemed to fix; and, even if such reasons did not exist, the gravity of the question and the special respect which provisions regulated by private civil legislation deserve would have induced the Government to submit the reform to the Cortes, notwithstanding its urgent need for the island of Cuba. The plan which is herewith presented has been compiled, with the full approval of the Committee on Codes for the Colonies, in its essential points as well as in the method adopted to facilitate parliamentary deliberations, and to reconcile formalities of law with the necessity so urgently impressed by Cuba. If the Cortes will condescend to pass this new law, containing all that has been approved by the Senate, for the Peninsula, as well as the changes derived from the Civil Code, and if His Majesty will sanction the same, the Colonies will enjoy in advance remedies which are for the most part desired by the whole national territory.

In accordance with these remarks, with the authority of His Majesty and with the approval of the Council of Ministers, the undersigned has the honor to submit for the approval of the Cortes the following

PROPOSED LAW.

Article first and last. The Government is hereby authorized to put into effect the law submitted by the Colonial Minister, with the approval of the Committee on Codes, amending the mortgage law for Cuba, Puerto Rico, and the Philippines.

Madrid, May 26, 1893.

The Colonial Minister,

ANTONIO MAURA Y MONTANER.

MORTGAGE LAW FOR THE COLONIES.

TITLE I.

INSTRUMENTS REQUIRING RECORD.

ARTICLE 1. Registries of real estate shall be located in all towns where they have been established by law. Registries can not be abolished nor created, nor can the present territorial limits of any one of them be changed, without provision of law.

In every Registry shall be recorded the instruments relative to the estates situated within their territorial limits. If an estate is situated within the limits of two or more Registries, it shall be recorded in all of them.

ART. 2. In the Registries mentioned in the preceding article shall be recorded:

1. Instruments transferring or declaring ownership of realty, or of property rights thereto. .

2. Instruments by which rights of use, use and occupancy, emphyteusis, mortgage, annuity (censo), servitudes, and any others by which estates are created, acknowledged, modified, or extinguished.

3. Instruments or contracts by virtue of which real property or property rights are conveyed to a person, although it is with the obligation of transferring them to others or of investing their value for specified purposes.

4. Writs declaring the legal incapacity for administration, or the presumption of death of absentees, or injunction, or in anyway altering the civil capacity of persons with regard to the free disposition of their property.

5. Contracts for the lease of real property for a period exceeding six years, or such contracts on which rent has been paid in advance for three or more years, or, if having neither of these conditions, they contain a special covenant by which record thereof is required.

6. Title deeds of real property or property rights owned or administered by the State, or by civil or ecclesiastical corporations, subject to the provisions of laws or regulations.

ART. 3. To permit the record of the title deeds mentioned in the preceding article, they must be in the shape of a public document, writ, or certified document, issued by a judicial authority or by the Government or its agents, in the form prescribed by the regulations.

Notwithstanding the provisions of the preceding paragraph, those who have the ownership or possession of property rights recorded in their favor, the individual value of which does not exceed 300 pesos, may alienate or mortgage them by appearing before the proper notary with the grantee or mortgagee and two witnesses. The original draft of the contract shall necessarily contain a description of the realty and the enumeration of liens or incumbrances, if there be any, the names and surnames, the status (whether married or single), profession, and residence of the grantor and of the grantee, as well as the consideration involved.

The original contract, which should be executed on official paper, must be recorded in the Registry of the notary certifying to it. The copy, executed on paper of the lowest class (or, if it has been made on common paper, a stamp of the same class will have to be affixed thereto), shall be presented to the Registry of property for record, as it must serve as the title of the grantee.

Partitions of inheritances, which do not exceed 2,500 pesos in value, may be effected by all the participants or their representatives appearing before a notary, who shall execute an instrument containing descriptions of the estates, their award to each interested person, the covenants and limitations with which they are made, and other necessary requisites regarding the personality of the interested persons, so that said instrument may be recorded. The said document shall have to be signed by all the interested parties, or by two witnesses procured for this purpose. If anyone of the interested parties should not know how or should not be able to sign, it shall be done in his name by either of the witnesses, the notary stating this circumstance in the instrument. Should the notary not be acquainted with the interested parties, he shall demand that two witnesses known to him shall identify them, who may be the same who take part in the execution of the instrument.

The duplicate of this instrument, a copy of which shall be given to each one of the interested parties, shall be their title for record, the original being filed in the notary's register.

When, according to law, an approval of the partition or awards is necessary, it shall be the duty of the notary, under his own responsibility, to send the original instrument to the Court of First Instance of the subdistrict, so that this requisite may be filled without any further delay than its posting in the office of the secretary of the court for the period of eight days. It shall then be returned, also officially and without charging any fees, to the notary who sent it, with a decree approving the partition.

Any objection made by one of the interested parties shall be heard before the same court in conformity with the regulations established for oral trials by the Law of Civil Procedure.

When, for the execution of the instrument referred to in the preceding paragraphs, a previous declaration of heirs is necessary, the notary shall demand of the interested parties the documents necessary to make said declaration, and the presence of the witnesses who shall testify as to the nonexistence of a will. It shall be his duty to send the record formed in this manner to the Court of First Instance, which, with the consent of the Department of Public Prosecution, shall thereupon issue the corresponding decree of heirship after such announcements or edicts as may be necessary, returning the original to the notary from whom it was received, who shall file it in his proper register, as has been before stated.

The fee for the above-mentioned procedure shall be 7.50 pesos; for the execution of the instrument of partition, if the total value of the estate does not exceed 1,000 pesos, the fee shall be 5 pesos; if the value exceeds 1,000 but is not more than 1,500, 7.50 pesos; from 1,500 to 2,000, 10 pesos; for the copies issued to each interested party 25 cents a folio shall be charged.

The paper to be used for the originals as well as the copies of the record above mentioned shall be stamped paper of the lowest class.

ART. 4. For the effects of this law, transferable public offices (oficios públicos) conferred by the Crown, securities of public debt, or shares of banks or mercantile companies, even if they are negotiable, and those of ordinary partnerships, whatever be their kind, shall not be considered as real property.

ART. 5. The documents or deeds mentioned in article 2, which have been executed in foreign countries, and which are effectual in Spain in accordance with the laws, and such decrees as are mentioned in No. 4 of the same article, issued by foreign courts, which must be complied with in the Kingdom in accordance with the Law of Civil Procedure, shall also be recorded in the Registry.

TITLE II.

RECORD, ITS METHOD AND ITS EFFECTS.

ART. 6. The record of instruments in the Registry may be demanded indiscriminately:

By the person conveying the interest;

By the person acquiring the same:

By any person interested in securing the interest which is to be recorded;

By the person who is legally authorized to represent any of the above.

ART. 7. When in any instrument or contract any property interest in real estate is reserved to persons who were not parties to the same, the notary who executes the deed, or, in the absence of a notary, the official who may issue it, shall require the record of the said property right whenever the interests of said persons appear from the instrument itself, or from the documents and proceedings upon which its execution was based.

If the instrument or contract is subject to record, and this has been requested, particular mention must be made therein of the property right reserved, and of the persons in whose favor the reservation has been made.

ART. 8. Each estate which is recorded for the first time in the Registries shall be marked with a distinct and correlative number.

The records corresponding to each estate shall be marked by another correlative and special numeration.

ART. 9. Every record made in the Registry shall contain the following details:

1. The nature, location, and bounds of the realty which is the subject of record, or which is affected by the interest which is to be recorded, its superficial area measured according to the standard used in the country, and its equivalent in the metrical system, and its name and number, if they appear in the deed.

2. The nature, extension, conditions, and liens of any kind, of the interest recorded and its value, if it appear in the deed.

3. The nature, extension, conditions, and liens of the interest on which is created that which is the subject of record.

4. The nature of the instrument which is to be recorded and its date.

5. The name and surname of the person, if it is an individual, or, if not, the name of the corporation, or the names of all the parties interested in whose favor the record is made.

6. The name and surname of the person, or the name of the corporation, or of the legal person who is the last owner of the interests or estates which are to be recorded.

7. The name and location of the court, notary, or official who executes the instrument which is to be recorded.

8. The date of the presentation of the instrument to the Registry, with a statement of the time.

9. The conformity of the record with the copy of the instrument from which it was taken, and if the latter is one of those which are to be kept in the office of the Registry, the *liber* in which it is entered will also be indicated.

10. The date of the record and the full signature of the Register.

ART. 10. In the record of contracts involving cash considerations or transfers thereof the amount involved shall be mentioned, as well as the manner in which the payment was made or agreed to.

ART. 11. If the record be one transferring ownership, it shall indicate whether the price of this transfer was paid for in cash or in installments; in the former case, if the whole price was paid or a part thereof, and in the latter, the manner and terms agreed to for payment.

Similar details shall be expressed if the transfer of ownership is made in consideration of an exchange, or awarded in payment, and whether either of the grantees is to allow the other any difference in money or goods.

ART. 12. The records of mortgage debts shall in every instance contain the value of the obligation secured and of the interest, if any has been stipulated, and if none has been stipulated, it shall not be considered secured by the mortgage according to the regulations prescribed by the present law.

ART. 13. Records of servitudes shall be made:

1. On the page reserved for record of servient estates.

2. On the page reserved for record of dominant estates.

ART. 14. The entries of trusts shall be made at once in the name of the trustees.

ART. 15. The recording of the decrees mentioned in No. 4 of article 2, and in article 5 of this law, and of the record of cautionary notices of the suits mentioned in No. 5 of article 42 shall clearly state the nature of the legal incapacity which appears from said decrees or suits.

ART. 16. The compliance or noncompliance with conditions precedent, and the nonfulfillment of conditions subsequent, or conditions involving recision, contained in recorded instruments or contracts, shall be recorded in the Registry by means of a marginal note.

The payment of any sum made by the grantee, after the record, on account of the purchase price or in full liquidation thereof, or to cover the difference between an exchange, or in the award in payment, shall also be recorded by means of a marginal note, provided the interested parties request it, or if it has been so ordered by the court or judge.

The fulfillment of conditions subsequent or conditions involving recision, shall appear by means of a new record in favor of the person having the right thereto.

ART. 17. After any instrument transferring the ownership or possession of realty, or of property rights thereto, has been recorded or a cautionary notice thereof made in the Registry, no other instrument of the name or of a previous date may be recorded or noted, by which the ownership of the same estate or property right is transferred or encumbered.

If only the presentation of the instrument transferring ownership or possession has been recorded, no other deed of the kind previously mentioned may be recorded or noted for the period of thirty days following the date of said record.

ART. 18. Registers shall determine, under their responsibility, the legality of the documents by virtue of which the record is requested, and the capacity of the parties interested by what appears from said documents.

All the documents issued by judicial authorities shall also be determined by them under their responsibility, and for the sole purpose of admitting, suspending, or refusing their record or entry.

There shall be no further remedies than those mentioned in this law against the suspension or refusal of a record or cautionary notice, judges or courts by virtue of judicial documents not being permitted to compel the Registers in any other manner to record or enter.

ART. 19. Should the Register perceive any error with regard to the legal form of the instrument, or as to the capacity of the parties thereto, he shall advise the persons requesting the record thereof, so that, if they wish it, they may withdraw the instrument and make the necessary corrections within the time of the effectiveness of the entry of presentation, according to article 17; and if they do not withdraw the instrument and correct the error to the satisfaction of the Register he shall return the document, so that the necessary steps may be taken without prejudice to making the cautionary notice required by article 42, No. 8, if it is expressly requested.

In case the cautionary notice is not made, the entry of presentation of the deed shall continue effectual during the thirty days above mentioned.

The regulations shall explicitly describe the manner of proceeding in cases in which the requested record or entry is suspended or refused, by virtue of documents issued by judicial authorities.

ART. 20. To record or enter instruments transferring or encumbering the ownership or possession of real property or property rights, the interest of the person conveying it, or in whose name the transfer or encumbrance is made, must be previously recorded.

Registers shall refuse to record said instruments as long as this requisite has not been complied with, being directly responsible for the damage they may cause third parties by the violation of this provision.

However, they may record without this requisite all deeds executed by persons who have acquired an interest in the same property before the day on which the mortgage law was put into operation, provided they justify their title with trustworthy documents, and the same interest is not recorded in favor of another person; but in the record requested the essential circumstances of said title will be indicated, which shall be taken from the documents necessary for this purpose.

Registers shall refuse the requested record, if said interest is recorded in favor of a person other than the one executing the transfer or encumbrance.

Should the interest mentioned not be recorded in favor of any other person, and it is not proven that the grantor acquired it before the date mentioned, the Registers shall enter a cautionary notice at the request of the interested party, which shall be effectual during the period stated in article 96 of this law.

ART. 21. Public copies of instruments or contracts which require record shall at least contain all the details which the record must contain, or otherwise be null, relating to the persons of the parties thereto, to the estates, or to the recorded interests.

The owners of the real property or property rights acquired by any general or special instrument which does not mention and describe them individually, may obtain their record by presenting said instrument with the document, if there be one, which proves that they are the ones to whom the transfer was made, justified by any other trustworthy document showing that the property which it is desired to record is embraced in said instrument.

ART. 22. The notary who omits anything preventing the entry of the instrument or contract, in accordance with the provisions of the preceding article, shall, if it is possible to do so, repair his omission by issuing a new deed at his own cost, and in any case indemnifying the interested parties for the damage caused by his error.

ART. 23. The instruments mentioned in articles 2 and 5 which are not duly recorded or entered in the Registry can not prejudice third persons.

The record of real property and property rights, acquired through an inheritance or legacy, shall not prejudice third persons until five years have elapsed since the date thereof, excepting in cases of testate or intestate inheritances, legacies and additions thereto (mejoras), when left to legal heirs.

In the award of specific realty in an inheritance or general assignment to a person having the right thereto, to a creditor, or to any third person, with the obligation of devoting its value to the payment of debts or charges on the same inheritance or general assignment, the conditions under which the property has been awarded shall be entered when it is recorded in the name of the person to whom the property has been awarded, and it shall have the effects which this law establishes in No. 1 of article 37.

The other property of the inheritance or general assignment shall by this act be relieved of all responsibility, although only to the prejudice of third persons, notwithstanding that the debts of the inheritance or general assignment appear in their records. When no specific property has been awarded for the payment of debts, all the property of the inheritance or general assignment shall be relieved of all responsibility to the prejudice of third persons, even when the registry shows the existence of debts.

ART. 24. The instruments recorded shall also be effectual against creditors specially privileged by common legislation.

ART. 25. Recorded instruments shall be effectual against third persons only from the day of record.

ART. 26. To determine which of two records, bearing the same date and relating to the same estate, shall have preference, the hour of the presentation of the respective instruments in the Registry shall be taken into consideration.

ART. 27. For the purposes of this law, those who have not participated in the recorded instrument or contract shall be considered as third persons.

ART. 28. The date of the entry of presentation, which must appear in the record itself, shall be considered the date thereof for all intents and purposes.

ART. 29. The ownership of any other property right which is expressly mentioned in the records or cautionary notices, although it does not appear in the Registry as a separate and special entry, shall be effectual against third persons from the date of the entry of presentation of the respective instrument.

The provisions of the preceding paragraph must not be understood as interfering with the obligation of specially recording the rights referred to, and with the responsibility incurred by persons who, in certain cases, must demand the record.

ART. 30. The records of the instrument mentioned in articles 2 and 5 shall be null if they do not contain the details mentioned in Nos. 1, 2, 3, 4, 5, 6, and 8 of article 9, and in No. 1 of article 13.

ART. 31. The nullity of the records treated of in the preceding article shall not prejudice any interest previously acquired by a third person, who was not a party to the recorded instrument or contract.

ART. 32. The record shall be understood to lack some of the details embraced in the numbers and articles mentioned in article 30, not only when all the requisites mentioned in each one of said numbers and articles is not embraced therein, but also when they have been expressed so inaccurately that a third person could thereby be led into error, as to the object of the fact itself, and suffer loss in consequence thereof.

When the inaccuracy is not material, as provided by the preceding article, or when the omission does not embrace all the details mentioned in some of the numbers and articles referred to, the record shall be declared null only when it causes some error or loss.

ART. 33. The record of instruments or contracts which are null in accordance with the law are not validated thereby.

ART. 34. Notwithstanding the statements contained in the preceding article, the instruments or contracts executed or covenanted by a person who, according to the Registry, has a right thereto, shall not be invalidated with regard to third persons, after they have once been recorded, although later the right of the person executing them is annulled or determined by virtue of a prior deed not recorded, or for reasons which do not clearly appear from the Registry.

Only by virtue of a recorded instrument may another later instrument, also recorded, be invalidated to the prejudice of third persons, with the exceptions mentioned in article 389.

The provisions of this article may at no time be applied to the instrument recorded in accordance with the provisions of article 390, unless the prescription has validated or secured the interest referred to therein.

ART. 35. A prescription which does not require a just title shall not prejudice third persons if its possessory title is not recorded.

Neither shall a third person be prejudiced by a prescription which requires a just title if the latter is not recorded.

In either case the time of the prescription shall begin from the date of the record.

As to the legal owner of the realty or interest which is being prescribed, the title shall be determined and the time computed in accordance with common law.

ART. 36. Suits for recision or determination of title shall not be instituted against third persons who have recorded the instruments of their respective interests in conformity with the provisions of this law.

ART. 37. Exceptions to the rule contained in the preceding article are:

1. Suits for recision or determination of title which are due to the causes plainly expressed in the Registry.

2. Suits for recision of conveyances made for the purpose of defrauding creditors in the following cases:

When the second conveyance has been made without consideration.

When the third person was a party to the fraud.

In both cases the third person shall not be prejudiced by any action for recision not brought within one year from the time of the fraudulent conveyance.

ART. 38. In consequence of the provisions of article 36, no instruments or contracts shall be annulled or rescinded to the prejudice of third persons who may have had their interests recorded for any of the following reasons:

1. For the revocation of gifts in such cases as are permitted by law, except when the donee does not comply with conditions entered in the Registry.

2. For the legal retraction of the sale, or the legal preference (tanteo) in an emphyteusis.

3. For not having paid the full price of the article sold, or a portion thereof, if it does not appear by the record that the payment has been postponed.

4. For the resale of an article, when either the sale or resale has not been recorded.

5. For willful damage (lesion) in cases 1 and 2 of article 1291 of the Civil Code.

6. For conveyances made for the purpose of defrauding creditors, with the exception of the cases mentioned in the preceding article.

7. For any other actions, which the laws or special statutes permit certain persons to bring for the purpose of rescinding contracts for reasons not specifically stated in the record.

In every case that the suit for recision or determination of title can not be instituted against the third person, in accordance with the provisions of this article, the corresponding personal action may be brought to recover from the person who may have been the cause thereof, indemnity for the injuries and damages suffered.

ART. 39. By a conveyance without consideration to defraud creditors in case 1, No. 2 of article 37, shall be understood not only the one by gift or cession of a right, but also any conveyance, creation, or renunciation which the debtor makes of some property right within the periods respectively mentioned in the common or in the proper commercial laws, for the recision of conveyances made to defraud creditors, provided

19539——2

there was no price or its equivalent, or any preexisting obligation which had fallen due.

ART. 40. In accordance with the provisions of the preceding article, and providing the circumstances mentioned exist, the following may be revoked:

1. Annuities (censos), emphyteusis, servitudes, uses, and other property rights created by the debtor.

2. The creation of dowries or gifts by reason of marriage, in favor of the wife, children, or strangers.

3. Conveyances of real property for the payment of debts which have not yet fallen due.

4. Voluntary mortgages created for the security of debts previously contracted without this guaranty, and which have not yet fallen due, provided the conditions of the principal obligation are not thereby encumbered.

5. Any contract by which the debtor transfers or renounces expressly or impliedly any property right.

It shall be understood that no price or its equivalent figures in said contracts, when the notary does not certify as to its delivery or if the contracting parties acknowledge that the delivery had previously taken place, and the fact is not proven or it is shown that it must be embraced in case No. 3 of this article.

ART. 41. The owner of the realty or of the property right shall be considered a party to the fraudulent conveyance in the second case, No. 2 of article 37:

1. When it is proven that he knew the purpose of making said conveyance, and that he was a party to it in the character of last owner or in any other capacity.

2. When he acquired his interest, either directly from the debtor or from a subsequent purchaser, for half or less than half its true value.

3. When any kind of false statements or subterfuge has been employed in the contract executed by the debtor, and it is proven that the owner had notice or took advantage thereof.

TITLE III.

CAUTIONARY NOTICES.

ART. 42. Cautionary notices of their respective interests in the corresponding public Registries may be demanded by:

1. The person who enters suit for the ownership of the real property, or for the creation, declaration, modification, or extinction of any property right.

2. The person who, in accordance with the law, obtains a writ of attachment against the real property of the debtor.

3. The person who, in any trial, obtains a decree against the defendant, which must be carried out in the manner prescribed by title 8 of the Law of Civil Procedure.

4. The person who enters a declaratory suit for the fulfillment of any obligation, and who, in accordance with the laws, obtains a decree ordering the sequestration or prohibiting the alienation of the real property.

5. The person who enters a suit for the purpose of obtaining any of the decrees mentioned in No. 4 of article 2 of this law.

6. The widower by the right granted him by article 838 of the Civil Code.

7. The legatee who, according to the law, has no right to institute testamentary proceedings.

8. The agricultural creditor, during the time the work lasts which is the object of the loan.

9. The person who presents an instrument to the Registry which can not be definitely recorded on account of some omission which may be repaired, or on account of the incapacity of the Register.

10. The person who in any other case has a right to demand a cautionary notice in accordance with the provisions of this law.

ART. 43. In the case of No. 1 of the preceding article, no cautionary notice may be made unless it is so ordered by a judicial decree issued at the instance of a person having a right thereto and by virtue of a document sufficient in the opinion of the judge.

In the case of No. 2 of the same article, the record shall be obligatory, according to the provisions of article 1435 of the Law of Civil Procedure, in force in the Philippines, and article 1451 of the law which is in force in Cuba and Puerto Rico.

In the case of No. 5 of the said preceding article, the entry must also be made by virtue of a judicial decree, which may be issued by reason of the duty to do so, when there are no persons requesting it, provided the court, in its opinion, deems said entry advisable to insure the effect of any judgment which may be rendered in the suit.

ART. 44. The creditor who obtains an entry in his favor in cases Nos. 2, 3, and 4, of article 42, shall have preference, only with regard to the property entered, over those who have another claim against the same debtor, contracted subsequently to said entry.

ART. 45. In the case No. 6 of article 42, the widower may demand a cautionary notice of the right of use which belongs to him, against all the realty of the inheritance, in accordance with the procedure indicated in articles 55, 56, and 57, of this law.

ART. 46. The legatee, who has no right, according to the law, to institute testamentary proceedings, may at any time request a cautionary notice against the goods bequeathed him, if they consist of specific personal property.

If the legacy is not specific, the legatee may demand a record of its value against any of the realty of the inheritance sufficient to cover it, within 180 days following the death of the testator.

In either case the entry shall be made by presenting in the Registry the instrument on which the interest of the legatee is based.

The legatee of specific personal property, or of credits, or annuities arising therefrom, can procure a cautionary notice against such property only.

ART. 47. The legatee of goods or money can not demand their entry against real property which has been expressly bequeathed to others.

ART. 48. No legatee of goods or money who has a cautionary notice in his favor can prevent another legatee of the same kind from obtaining another entry within the period allowed by law in his favor against the property which has already been entered.

ART. 49. If the heir wishes to enter, in his name, the goods inherited within the 180 days mentioned, and there is no legal obstacle thereto, he may do so, provided that all the legatees previously renounce, by public deed, their right to entry, or, in case no express renunciation is made, the same legatees are notified thirty days beforehand of the request of the heir, so that they may make use of their privilege within said period, if they wish to do so.

This notification shall be made in accordance with the provisions of articles 254, 255, 258, and 509 of the Law of Civil Procedure in force in the Philippines, and 270, 271, 274, and 525 of the one in force in Cuba and Puerto Rico.

If the identity of the legatees is in doubt, the judge or court shall order that a cautionary notice of their legacy be made, either at the instance of the heir himself, or at that of any other interested person, or by reason of a special duty.

The heir who requests a record in his favor of the property inherited, within the 180 days referred to, may at once have a cautionary notice thereof made.

This entry shall not be converted into a definite record until the legatees have expressly or impliedly renounced the entry of their legacies, and it shall be canceled with regard to the property against which the same legatees request a cautionary notice to be filed in accordance with their rights.

ART. 50. The legatee who obtains a cautionary notice shall be preferred to the creditors of the heir who may have accepted the inheritance without the benefit of inventory, and to any other who, subsequent to the date of said entry, acquires some interest in the property entered; but it is to be understood that this preference is only in so far as the value of said property is concerned.

ART. 51. The cautionary notice shall give preference, with regard to the value of the entered property, to the legatees who may have made use of their right within the 180 days mentioned in article 46 over those who do not make use of their privilege within the same period.

Those who have secured said entry within this period shall have no preference over each other, but without prejudice to that corresponding to the specific legatee, in accordance with common law, over other legatees, in this instance as well as in the case of his not having requested its entry.

ART. 52. The legatee who is not specific, and allows the period mentioned in article 46 to elapse without making use of his privilege, may only later on demand a cautionary notice against the property of the inheritance which is in the hands of the heir; but this shall have no effect against any person who may have previously acquired and recorded some interest in the inherited property.

ART. 53. The legatee who, after the 180 days have elapsed, should request a cautionary notice against the hereditary property which is in the hands of the heir, shall not thereby acquire any preference over the other legatees who may have omitted this formality, nor shall he gain any other advantage than that of recovering his legacy before any creditor of the heir subsequently acquiring some interest in the entered property.

ART. 54. An entry, requested after this period has elapsed, may be made against property noted within this period in favor of another legatee, provided they are in possession of the heir; but the legatee who obtains it can recover his legacy only to the extent of the value of the property after the claims of those who had their entry made within said period have been satisfied.

ART. 55. A cautionary notice of legacies and of agricultural loans made shall not be judicially decreed without previous proceedings and hearing of those who may have any interest in preventing it.

ART. 56. The cautionary notice of legacies may be made by virtue of an agreement between the parties or by a judicial decree.

ART. 57. When the entry must be made by virtue of a judicial decree, the legatee shall appear before the judge or court having jurisdiction of the will establishing his right, presenting the documents on which it is founded, and specifying the property which he desires to have entered. The court, in an oral trial, and in accordance with the statements of the heir and said legatee, shall render a decision, either refusing or complying with the request, in accordance with the procedure established by chapter 4, title 2, book 2 of the Law of Civil Procedure.

In the latter case it shall specify the property which is to be entered, and shall send the respective communication to the Register, inclosing a literal copy of its decision, for compliance.

An appeal may be taken from this decision to the Audiencia of the district.

ART. 58. If the entry has been judicially requested by one legatee and a second one appears with a similar claim on the same property, he shall also be heard at the trial.

ART. 59. The agricultural creditor may request an entry against the estate which is the subject of the loan for the amounts which he advanced in one payment or in successive ones, presenting the written contract he may have in any legal manner made with the debtor.

This entry shall have, with regard to the agricultural loan, all the effects of a mortgage.

ART. 60. It shall not be necessary that the instruments by virtue of which the cautionary notice of agricultural loans is requested should specify the exact amount of money or effects these credits consist of, and it shall be sufficient for them to contain enough details to liquidate them when the works contracted for are terminated.

ART. 61. If the estate which is the subject of the agricultural loan should be subject to recorded real property agreements, the entry can only be made by virtue of a unanimous agreement, by means of a public instrument between the owner and the persons in whose favor said agreements are created, on the object of the improvement itself, and the value of the estate before beginning the works, or by virtue of a judicial decree issued in a proceeding for the purpose of fixing said value, and in which all the parties indicated are cited.

ART. 62. If any of those in whose favor the real-property agreements mentioned in the preceding article are entered is not a person whose identity is known, or is absent and his residence is unknown, or he refuses his consent thereto, the entry may only be made by virtue of a judicial decree.

ART. 63. The value at which the estate which is the subject of the agricultural loan is appraised, before the work is begun, shall appear in the record of the debt.

ART. 64. The persons in whose favor property rights are created in the estate which is the subject of the agricultural loan, the value of which appears in the form prescribed by the preceding articles, shall reserve their rights of preference with regard to the agricultural creditor, but only to the extent of the appraised value of the estate.

The agricultural creditor shall be considered as a mortgagee, with respect to the excess of the value of the estate over the obligations mentioned above, and in any case, with respect to the difference between the price at which the estate was appraised before the improvement and its value at the time of the judicial conveyance.

ART. 65. Errors which may be remedied are such as affect the validity of the instrument itself, without necessarily producing the nullity of the obligation created thereby.

Should the instrument contain any of these errors, the Register shall suspend its record, and shall enter a cautionary notice thereof if the person presenting the instrument request it.

Errors which can not be corrected are such as necessarily produce the nullity of the obligation.

If the instrument should not contain any error of this kind, its record will be refused, and no cautionary notice can be entered.

ART. 66. The parties interested may object to administrative officers against the decision respecting the instrument made by the Register, without prejudice to applying, if they wish to do so, to the courts of justice to discuss and contend among themselves regarding the validity or nullity of the documents or of the obligation. In case record is suspended on account of errors in the instrument which may be corrected, and the cautionary notice is not requested, the interested parties may correct the errors within the thirty days during which the entry of presentation is effective. If the cautionary notice is entered, they may be corrected during the time the latter remains in force, according to article 96.

If record has been refused, and the interested person should enter a suit before the courts of justice to have established the validity of the instrument or obligation, within the thirty days following the date of the record of presentation, he may demand entry of a cautionary notice of his suit, and the entry shall be antedated to conform with the date of the record of presentation.

After said period the cautionary notice of the suit shall be effectual only from its date.

In the case of appealing to administrative officers against the decision respecting the instrument, all the periods mentioned in the two preceding paragraphs shall be suspended from the day the appeal is entered until its final resolution.

ART. 67. In case an entry is made because the record can not take place on account of an error which can be corrected, the interested party may demand that the Register give him a copy of said entry, authenticated by his signature, in which shall appear whether there are pending or not any other instruments relative to the same realty, and, if so, what they are.

ART. 68. Decrees ordering or refusing a cautionary notice in cases 1, 5, and 6 of article 42 may be appealed from for review only (un solo efecto).

In case No. 7 of the same article the decree may be appealed from for review and also to stay proceedings (ambos efectos) when the person who has some prior property right in the recorded realty has opposed the entry.

ART. 69. The person who may demand a cautionary notice of an interest and should not do so within the period prescribed for this purpose can not have it entered subsequently in his favor to the prejudice of a third person who may have recorded the same interest, having acquired it from a person who, according to the Registry, was competent to convey it.

ART. 70. When the cautionary notice of an interest is converted into a definite record of the same, it shall be effectual from the date of its entry.

ART. 71. The real property or property rights which are entered may be conveyed or encumbered, but without prejudice to the right of the person in whose favor the entry was made.

If the real property or property rights of which cautionary entries have been made in accordance with article 42, Nos. 2 and 3, should be awarded to a claimant by virtue of a judgment rendered in a suit, or if it were necessary to offer them at public sale, a notice of said award or advertisement shall be transmitted to the person who may have acquired said property or rights during the pendency of the suit.

Said notice must be issued at the instance of the plaintiff after the award has been finally decreed or before the sale in the judicial proceedings takes place, observing the provisions of articles 260 to 269 of the Law of Civil Procedure in force in the Antilles, and articles 244 to 253 of the one in force in the Philippines.

After the notice referred to in the preceding paragraph has been made the person notified may free the property in question by paying the amount mentioned in the entry to cover principal and costs; this must not be construed as meaning that he is obliged to pay a larger sum than that mentioned in the entry. Should he not do so within ten days, the record of his ownership shall be cancelled in the Registry, as well as any other record that has been made after the entry, for which purpose the respective order shall be transmitted to the Register at the instance of the purchaser at the auction, or of the person to whom it has been awarded.

If the conveyance executed and recorded during the pendency of the suit relates to an estate, the ownership of which is demanded by virtue of a claim, a cautionary notice of which has been made in accordance with No. 1 of article 42 of this law, a certified copy of the final judgment in favor of the ownership of the plaintiff shall be a valid title deed by virtue of which this record may be canceled.

Final decrees of prohibition or declaring the legal incapacity of some person for administration, or by which his civil status with reference to the free disposition of his property is modified, shall be sufficient documents for the cancellation of records of conveyances executed during the period of the pendency of the suit instituted by the person who has been declared incapacitated, provided a cautionary notice of the claim, which is the basis of the decree, shall have been previously made in accordance with the provisions of article 42, No. 5.

ART. 72. Cautionary notices shall embrace the details required for record by articles 9, 10, 11, 12, and 13, in so far as they appear in the deeds or documents presented at the time said entries are requested.

Such as are caused by writs of attachment or sequestration shall express the reason for which they were granted and the amount of the obligation involved.

ART. 73. Any judicial decree ordering a cautionary notice, shall express the details which the latter must contain, according to the provisions of the preceding article, if it so appear from the deeds or documents, which were examined and were the basis of said decree.

When the entry must embrace all the property of a person, as in cases of incapacity or other similar cases, the Register shall enter all that are recorded in favor of such person.

In this case the property which is not recorded may also be entered, provided the judge or court so order it, and a previous record is made in favor of the owner of the property encumbered by said entry.

ART. 74. If the instruments or documents, by virtue of which the cautionary notice is requested judicially or extra judicially, should not contain the details required to make it valid, such details shall be stated by the interested parties in the petition in which they solicit the entry by common consent. Should there be no agreement, the person requesting the entry shall mention these details in the document in which he solicits it, and after hearing the other interested party as to its accuracy, the judge or court will decide as they deem proper.

ART. 75. Cautionary notices shall be made in the same part of the book where the record would be made, if the right entered should be converted into a recorded right.

ART. 76. A cautionary notice shall be null when the estate or interest entered, or the persons whom the entry concerns, or its date, can not be identified therefrom.

TITLE IV.

CANCELLATION OF THE RECORD AND OF THE ENTRY OF CAUTIONARY NOTICES.

ART. 77. Records are not extinguished as to third persons except by their cancellation, or by a record of the transfer of the ownership or property right recorded, to another person.

ART. 78. Cancellation of records or of cautionary notices may be total or partial.

ART. 79. A total cancellation may be demanded, and should be ordered in a proper case:

1. When the realty, which is the subject of the record, is completely extinguished.

2. When the recorded interest is also completely extinguished.

3. When the instrument, by virtue of which the record was made, is declared null.

4. When the nullity of the instrument is declared, because some essential requisite is lacking, in conformity with the provisions of article 30.

ART. 80. A partial cancellation may be demanded and should be decreed in a proper case:

1. When the realty, which is the subject of the record or cautionary notice, is diminished.

2. When the interest recorded is diminished in favor of the owner of the encumbered estate.

ART. 81. The enlargement of any recorded interest shall be the subject of a new entry, in which reference shall be made to the interest enlarged.

ART. 82. The records or cautionary notices made by virtue of a public document can not be canceled except by a final decree, from which there is no appeal in cassation pending, or by any other authenticated instrument or document, in which the person in whose favor the record or entry has been made, or his legal representative or attorney signifies his consent to the cancellation.

Notwithstanding the provisions of the preceding paragraph, the records or entries referred to therein may be canceled without the requisites mentioned, when the interest recorded is extinguished by a declaration of law, or as a result of the recorded deed itself.

The records and entries made by virtue of judicial decrees may only be canceled by a final decree, in which the facts provided by the first paragraph of this article appear.

Records made to account for sums represented by negotiable instruments may be canceled through the presentation of a document executed by those who collected the debts, and from which it must appear that at the time of its execution the negotiable instruments were canceled, or by a petition signed by these parties and the debtor, to which the instruments referred to will be attached, duly perforated. If some of them have been lost, there shall be presented with the document or petition a copy of the judicial decree declaring their cancellation. The register must convince himself of the authenticity of the signatures and the identity of the persons who make the request.

Records made to account for sums represented by instruments executed to bearer can not be canceled if the extinction of all the secured obligations can not be proven, unless a copy of the judicial decree declaring the extinction of said obligations is presented.

In the case mentioned in the preceding paragraph, in order to issue the judicial decree, four calls of those having a right to oppose the cancellation must be made by means of public notices and advertisements in the official papers, each one for the period of six months.

ART. 83. If a record or entry has been created by virtue of a judicial decree, and the parties interested agree in a legal manner to cancel it, they shall apply to the judge or court of competent jurisdiction by means of a document expressing their wishes, and after its contents have been ratified, if there is or can be no prejudice against third persons, a decree ordering the cancellation shall be issued.

The judge or court shall also issue a similar decree, when it is deemed advisable, although the person in whose favor the entry or record has been made does not consent to the cancellation.

If the record or entry has been created by means of a public document and its cancellation is ordered, the person whom said cancellation prejudices not consenting thereto, the other interested party may enter a declaratory suit therefor.

ART. 84. The judge or court, or the one which has legally succeeded it in such matters, which may have ordered an entry of a cautionary notice, or its conversion into a definite record, shall be competent to order its cancellation.

ART. 85. A cautionary notice shall be canceled, not only when the interest entered is extinguished, but also when it is respectively agreed to in the document or ordered in the decree that it be converted into a definite record.

If the entry has been made without a public document, and it is to be canceled without converting it into a definite record, the cancellation may also be made by means of documents similar to those which were presented when the entry was requested.

ART. 86. An entry in favor of a legatee who is not specific, shall be extinguished one year after its date.

If a legacy is not demandable at the end of ten months, the cautionary notice shall be considered effectual for two months longer, during which time it may be demanded.

ART. 87. If, before the cautionary notice is extinguished, it appears inefficient for the security of the legacy, on account of the liens or special conditions of the property entered, the legatee may demand that another be created against different property in the inheritance, provided such exists on which such incumbrance may be charged.

ART. 88. The legatee of rents or periodical annuities, absolutely imposed by the testator on any heir or on other legatees, but without declaring this obligation a personal one, shall have a right, within the period fixed in article 86, to demand that the cautionary notice which he may have made of his claim be converted into a record of mortgage.

ART. 89. The heir or legatee who has been charged with the annuity must create the mortgage mentioned in the preceding article on the same property which has been entered, if it is awarded to him, or on any other real property of the estate which may be awarded to him.

The choice, in any case, lies with the encumbered heir or legatee, and the person receiving the annuity must accept the mortgage offered by the former, provided it is sufficient and on property of the estate.

ART. 90. The person receiving the annuity, who has not filed a cautionary notice, may also, at any time, demand a record of his mortgage interest in the property of the estate which is in the possession of the heir, or which may have been awarded to the specially charged legatee or heir, provided he can do so by means of an efficient cautionary notice in accordance with the provisions of the preceding article.

This entry will only be effectual from its date.

ART. 91. The person receiving the annuity, who may have obtained a cautionary notice, can not demand a mortgage on any other property than that entered, if it is sufficient to secure the legacy. Should it not be sufficient, he may demand the creation of a mortgage on other property of the estate; but in the latter case he must act in conformity with the provisions contained in the second paragraph of the preceding article.

ART. 92. An entry in favor of an agricultural creditor shall be extinguished sixty days after the completion of the work which was the subject of the loan.

ART. 93. An agricultural creditor may convert his cautionary notice into a mortgage record if at the end of the period mentioned in the preceding article his loan has not been repaid entirely, the time stipulated in the contract not having expired.

If the time stipulated for the payment has expired, the creditor may either extend it by converting the entry into a mortgage record, or may demand immediate payment, for which purpose the entry will have the effect of a mortgage.

ART. 94. To convert an entry of an agricultural credit into a record of mortgage, the former shall be liquidated, if it is not already so, and a public deed shall be executed.

ART. 95. Any questions which may arise between the creditor and the debtor as to the liquidation of the agricultural loan, or regarding the creation of the mortgage, shall be decided by means of a declaratory suit. During the trial and settlement of this suit the cautionary notice shall remain in force and effect.

ART. 96. An entry demanded because a record could not be made on account of errors which can be corrected in the deed presented, shall become null sixty days after its date.

This period may be extended to one hundred and eighty days for just cause, and by virtue of an administrative resolution of the president of the Audiencia of the district, provided the deed presented does not emanate from a judicial decree, in which case the time can only be extended by another similar decree.

ART. 97. The cancellation of the records of cautionary notices does not in and of itself extinguish, with regard to the parties, the interests recorded which it effects; but when it has been made without any apparent cause for annulment, such as those mentioned in the following article, it shall have all its effects with regard to third persons, who, by reason thereof, may have acquired or recorded any interest, although later it is annulled for some reason which does not clearly appear from the said record of cancellation.

ART. 98. The cancellation shall be void:

1. When it does not clearly show what record or entry has been cancelled.

2. When it does not contain the names of the parties thereto, of the notary, or in a proper case the judge or court, and the date of the execution or delivery of the deed, by virtue of which the cancellation was made.

3. When it does not express the name of the person at whose instance or with whose consent the cancellation was made.

4. When the cancellation is made in the name of a person other than the one in whose favor the record or entry is made, and it does not appear therein by what authority said person acted.

5. When a partial cancellation does not specify clearly what part of the realty has disappeared, or what part of the obligation is extinguished and what still remains.

6. When the cancellation having taken place by virtue of the record or entry of a private document, the Register does not certify that he

is acquainted with the persons signing the same, or with the witnesses, in default of the former.

7. When the date of the presentation of the instrument by virtue of which the cancellation was ordered or agreed to, is not contained in the Registry.

ART. 99. The cancellation may be declared null, but not to the prejudice of third persons, in accordance with the provisions of article 97:

1. When the instrument by virtue of which it was made is declared false, null, or insufficient.

2. When it has been effected through error or fraud.

3. When an incompetent judge or court ordered it.

ART. 100. Registers shall determine under their responsibility, the legality of documents by virtue of which cancellation is requested, and the capacity of the parties thereto.

ART. 101. They shall determine in the same manner documents issued by judicial authorities, for the sole purpose of making or not making the cancellation of some record in the Registry.

Against these determinations, and those mentioned in the preceding article, the remedies mentioned in article 66 of this law may be taken.

ART. 102. The Register shall at once make the cancellation upon the president declaring the competency of the judge.

When the judge is not considered competent, the same Register shall communicate this decision to the person interested, returning the documents.

ART. 103. An appeal may be taken to the Audiencia from the decision of the president by the judges as well as by the parties interested, who, after a a hearing, shall determine what it may deem just.

A remedy by cassation may be had as respects the decision of the Audiencia.

ART. 104. The cancellation of any record must necessarily contain the following facts:

1. The kind of document by virtue of which the cancellation is made.

2. The date of the document and of its presentation to the Registry.

3. The name of the judge, court, or official who may have issued it, or the notary before whom it was executed.

4. The names of the parties interested in the records.

5. The manner in which the cancellation was made.

TITLE V.

MORTGAGES.

SECTION 1.—*Mortgages in general.*

ART. 105. A mortgage, directly and primarily, subjects the property on which it is imposed, no matter who may be its owner, to the fulfillment of the obligation for the security of which it was constituted.

ART. 106. The following only are mortgageable:
1. Real property.
2. Property rights in the realty, alienable in accordance with the laws.

ART. 107. The following are mortgageable, but with such restrictions as are hereinafter expressed:

1. A building erected on ground belonging to another, which, if mortgaged by the person who constructed it, shall be without prejudice to the right of the owner of the ground, this incumbrance being only secured by the interest which the person who constructed the building has therein.

2. The right of use, the mortgage being extinguished if the use terminates by an act independent of the will of the grantee. If it is terminated by his will, the mortgage shall be effectual until the obligation secured is fulfilled, or until such time as the use would naturally have terminated had the act not occurred which put an end thereto.

3. The mere ownership, in which case, if the use is merged with it in the person of the owner, the mortgage shall not only be maintained, but shall also extend to the use itself, unless the contrary has been agreed to.

4. Property already mortgaged, even if it was agreed not to mortgage it again, provided the preference is reserved, which the creditors in whose favor the prior mortgages are created have in the collection of their loans.

5. Surface, pasture, water, timber, and other similar property rights, provided the interests of other owners in common of the property are reserved.

6. Railroads, canals, bridges, and other works destined for the public service the operation of which the Government has granted for ten or more years, and the buildings or lands which, although not directly and exclusively used for said service, belong to private parties, provided they have been added to those works; but the mortgage shall be dependent on the determination of the right of the owner of the concession.

7. Property belonging to persons not having the free disposition thereof, in the cases and with the formalities which the laws prescribe for its alienation.

8. The interest in a voluntary mortgage, but the said mortgage shall be dependent on the determination of the said interest.

9. Property sold under a covenant to reconvey, or similar agreement, if the purchaser or his attorney limits the mortgage to the amount he would receive in case the sale is decided upon, a notice of the contract being given to the vendor, so that if the property is redeemed before the mortgage is canceled he shall not return the price without the knowledge of the creditor, provided no judicial order has been issued to that effect, or if the vendor or his agent mortgages the value of the property and also the amount which the purchaser would realize if the sale is decided on; but in the latter case the creditor can not proceed against the property mortgaged without previously redeeming it, in the name

of the debtor, within the period the latter has a right to do so, advancing the sum which may be necessary for this purpose.

10. Property in litigation, if a cautionary notice has been made of the claim which is the basis of the litigation, or if it appears in the record, that the creditors had knowlege of the suit, but in either case, the mortgage shall depend upon the decision of the suit, without prejudicing the rights of the persons interested therein, with the exception of those of the mortgagor.

ART. 108. The following are not mortgageable:

1. Growing crops and unpaid rents, separated from the estate which produces them.

2. Chattels permanently located in buildings, either useful or ornamental, or for the service of some industry, unless they are mortgaged together with said building.

3. Public offices conferred by the Crown (oficios públicos).

4. Bonds of the State debt, or of provinces or towns, and the obligations and stocks in banks, corporations, or companies of any kind.

5. The property right in things, which, although they will be owned in the future, are not yet recorded in the name of the person who will have a right to own them.

6. Servitudes, unless they are mortgaged together with the dominant estate, and excepting in any case that of water, which may be mortgaged.

7. The right of use which the law allows fathers or mothers in the property of their children and the surviving spouse in the property of the deceased.

8. Use and occupation.

9. Mines, if a definite title thereto has not yet been obtained, even if they are situated within one's own property.

ART. 109. The owner of property which is subject to pending conditions subsequent may mortgage or convey the same, provided the rights of the person interested in said conditions is not prejudiced, an express reserve of the rights referred to being made in the record.

If the pending condition subsequent should affect the whole property mortgaged, the latter can not be conveyed to collect the debt until said condition has been fulfilled and the realty passes to the absolute ownership of the debtor, but the income to which the latter is entitled shall at once be applied to the payment of the debt.

When the condition subsequent affects only a portion of the property mortgaged it must be judicially conveyed, together with said condition subsequent, to which the ownership of the debtor is subject, and the selling price, besides the income he is entitled to, being applied to the payment.

If, before the sale takes place, the debtor acquires the absolute ownership in the property mortgaged, the creditor has a right of action against it, and may demand that it be conveyed for the payment.

The provisions of this article may be applied to the property possessed, with a pending right of subrogation in favor of persons who may not have consented to the mortgage of said property.

ART. 110. A mortgage extends to natural increase, improvements, growing crops, and rents not collected when the obligation falls due, and the value of indemnities allowed or due the owner for insurance on the property mortgaged, or by virtue of condemnation by right of eminent domain.

ART. 111. In accordance with the provisions of the preceding article, the following shall be considered mortgaged together with the estate, provided they belong to the owner of the estate, although they are not mentioned in the contract:

1. Chattels permanently located in a building, either useful or ornamental, or for the service of some industry, even though they were placed there after the creation of the mortgage.

2. Improvements consisting of new plantings, works of irrigation and drainage, repairs, works for safety or alterations, comfort, ornamentation or raising of buildings, and any other similar works, which do not consist of additions to the land, except natural accretions, or in the new construction of buildings, where previously none existed.

3. Crops, which at the time the obligation falls due, are growing on the trees and plants, or have already been harvested, but not yet removed or warehoused.

4. Rents due and not yet paid, whatever may be the reason they have not been collected, and such as shall have to be paid until the creditor has recovered his whole credit.

5. Indemnities awarded or due the owner of the mortgaged realty, either for the insurance thereof or for the crops, provided the damage occurred after the creation of the mortgage, or on account of condemnation of the land by the right of eminent domain.

ART. 112. When the mortgaged estate passes into the hands of a third party, the mortgage shall not extend to the chattels permanently located in the buildings, nor to the improvements which do not consist in repairs, works for security or alterations, provided the costs thereof have been defrayed by the new owner, nor to growing crops and rents due, which are the property of the latter.

If some portion of the ground of an estate encumbered by prior mortgages passes into the hands of a third person, and it appears by the Registry that it does not contain any machinery, chattel, object, or construction of any kind, said portion of the estate shall continue subject to prior mortgages on the estate; but the third person may remove, whenever it is convenient for him to do so, any machinery, object, chattel, or construction which he may have brought or placed there, according to the circumstances, judicial proceedings against such additions being prohibited, and it not being lawful, when the estate and the portion sold is attached or sold at a public sale by other previous creditors of record, to demand the retention of such additions, whatever may be

33

their character. Prior mortgagees shall be notified of the record of the sale.

ART. 113. The owner of the accessions or improvements which are not considered mortgaged according to the provisions of the first paragraph of the preceding article, may demand their value or retain the objects of which they consist, if this can be done without depreciating the value of the rest of the property; but in the former case he can not prevent the fulfillment of the principal obligation under the pretext of enforcing his right, being obliged to recover what is due him for the price of the property itself when it is conveyed for the payment of the debt.

ART. 114. A mortgage created in favor of an interest-paying debt shall secure to the prejudice of third persons, besides the capital, only the interest for the two years last past and such part as is due for the current year.

ART. 115. After three years have elapsed from the time the loan began to accumulate interest which remains unpaid, the creditor may demand that the mortgage created be enlarged on the same mortgaged property, for the purpose of securing the interest corresponding to the first of said years, but only in case the obligation to pay part of the interest is past due and the debtor has failed to satisfy it.

If the creditor makes use of his right after said three years have elapsed, he may demand that a mortgage be extended to cover all the interest which at the time of said extension was not covered by the first mortgage; but this can in no case prejudice a mortgage created in favor of a person who had previously and after the two years acquired an interest in the mortgaged property.

Should the debtor not consent to said mortgage extension the creditor may demand it in a declaratory action and have a cautionary notice of the alleged claim entered.

ART. 116. If the mortgaged estate does not belong to the debtor, the creditor can not demand that the extension of the mortgage mentioned in the preceding article be created; but he has the same right of action with regard to the other real property which the said debtor possesses, and which he can mortgage.

ART. 117. The creditor, in case of annuities (censos) in arrears, can not proceed against the estate thus encumbered by the annuity (censo) to the prejudice of another mortgagee or subsequent annuitant, except in the manner and with the restrictions mentioned in articles 114 and 115; but he may demand a mortgage in those cases, and with the limitations which a mortgagee has a right to, according to the preceding article, whoever may be the owner of the estate encumbered by the annuity (censo).

ART. 118. When an estate on which an emphyteusis has been given has incurred forfeiture according to the laws, it shall pass into the hands of the immediate owner of the property, with the mortgages or incum-

19539——3

brances on the realty, constituted by the grantor of the emphyteusis, but all interests of said immediate owner being reserved at all times.

ART. 119. When several estates are mortgaged together to satisfy one debt only, the sum or portion of the incumbrance for which each estate is to be responsible shall be determined.

ART. 120. After the portion of the debt for which each mortgaged estate must be responsible is entered in the record, they can not be proceeded against to the prejudice of third persons, except for the amount for which they are respectively responsible and the corresponding interest in accordance with the provisions contained in preceding articles.

ART. 121. The provisions of the preceding article shall not be understood as prejudicing the rights of the creditor, if the mortgage does not satisfy the total amount of the debt, to proceed to recover the difference against the other mortgaged property which the debtor still owns, but without preference as to said difference over those who may have acquired some real interest in the property after the mortgage was recorded.

ART. 122. The mortgage shall continue intact as long as it is not canceled on all the property mortgaged, even if the obligation secured is reduced, and on any other portion of the same property which is retained, although the remainder has disappeared, but without prejudice to the provisions contained in the following two articles.

ART. 123. If a mortgaged estate is divided into two or more parts, the mortgage debt shall not be distributed among them unless the creditor and the debtor voluntarily agree to do so. If this distribution does not take place, the creditor may proceed for the whole of the sum guaranteed against any of the new estates into which the first one was divided, or against all of them simultaneously.

ART. 124. If a mortgage created for the security of a debt is distributed among various estates and the portion of the debt which is due from any of the estates has been paid, the interested party may demand a partial cancellation of the mortgage with regard to said estate. If the portion of the debt paid has been applied to the discharge of one or the other of the encumbered estates, not being less than the sum for which each is responsible, the debtor may select the one which is to be redeemed.

ART. 125. If there is only one estate mortgaged, or being several and the responsibility of each one is not stated on account of the occurrence of the case mentioned in article 123, the discharge can not be demanded of any portion of the mortgaged property, no matter what portion of the debt has been satisfied by the debtor.

In the case of one or several estates being encumbered by mortgage debts of various creditors, and they are sold or awarded for the payment of the first creditor in such manner that the value of what is sold or awarded does not equal or exceed the mortgage debt which is liquidated, the remaining debts shall be, by act and right, considered canceled, and will therefore be canceled in the registry after the proper order of the court for the sale or award, and the reasons therefor are filed referring to the instrument which created the solvency of the preferred debt, all subsequent records of annuities (censos) or mortgages and records of attachment also made subsequently, thus leaving the estate or estates which have been conveyed or awarded free from all incumbrances.

This shall be without prejudice to other rights and actions which the remaining creditors may exercise against the debtor in accordance with the laws.

Art. 126. A mortgage created by a person who has no right to do so, according to the Registry, shall not be valid, even if the mortgagor subsequently acquires said right.

Art. 127. In the mortgage shall appear the value of the estate as appraised by the contracting parties, which shall serve as a basis for the only judicial sale which can take place, if the period of the loan having expired, it does not appear in the Registry of property that said loan has been paid.

Art. 128. The judicial procedure before the public sale shall consist in the presentation, by the creditor, of a document to the court of competent jurisdiction in the place in which the property is situated, accompanied by the instrument constituting the debt, with a note of the record, and a certificate from the Register of property testifying that the mortgage lien does not appear canceled in his books at the end of said period.

Payment shall be demanded of the debtor if he resides in the place in which the estate is situated, or if his domicile is known; otherwise it shall be sufficient to notify the person in charge of the estate in any legal capacity, so that he may inform the owner of the demand.

Thirty days after this demand the orders shall be published in the Gazette (Gaceta) of the proper island, stating the condition of the title deeds, the public sale taking place twenty days after said publication. If there is no bidder the claimant may demand that the property be awarded to him, being responsible for all prior liens, if there be any.

When an estate is sold at public auction at the instance of a second or subsequent mortgagee, or common creditors, the sale shall be declared null and void if a sufficient sum is not offered to cover all previously recorded debts, including the interest which it appears is stipulated according to the Registry. Any subsequent sales which they may deem advisable may take place at the cost of the claimants, providing they prove by a certificate from the Registry that they have not as yet been paid.

The estate proceeded against shall not be responsible for any costs which may be incurred, if the amount indispensable for this purpose is not entered in the Registry.

In the regulations for the execution of this law, the other details for this summary proceeding shall be determined.

ART. 129. If, before the creditor collects his interests in the mortgaged estate it should pass into the hands of a third person, all the measures prescribed in the preceding article shall have to be instituted against the latter, who is subrogated to the person of the debtor.

ART. 130. The provisions of the two preceding articles may also be applied to the case when an installment of the principal or interest has not been paid, due at different periods, if one of them lapses without the debtor fulfilling his obligation, provided said stipulation is recorded in the Registry.

ART. 131. If for the payment of one of the installments of the capital or interest it should be necessary to convey the mortgaged estate, and other installments of the obligation shall still remain due, the sale shall take place, and the estate shall be transferred to the purchaser with the proper mortgage for the portion of the debt which has not yet been satisfied, which portion with the interest will be deducted from the price.

If the purchaser does not desire the estate with this lien, the value thereof with the proper interest shall be deposited, to be paid to the creditor when the pending payments fall due.

ART. 132. A person who either may have acquired only the use or some interest in the mortgaged estate, or the title or direct ownership of the property, the correlative interest remaining in the debtor shall be considered a third party in interest, for all the purposes of article 129. If there should be more than a third party in interest, because one person had the title or direct ownership and another the use of, or some interest in, the mortgaged estate, the summons shall be served on the person in charge of the estate.

ART. 133. In no case shall the summary proceedings be suspended, on account of the objections of a third person, if they are not founded on a deed which has been previously recorded, nor by the death of the debtor, nor that of the third party owning the estate, nor by a declaration of bankruptcy, nor by the general assignment proceedings of creditors against any of them.

ART. 134. A foreclosure shall be prescribed after twenty years, computed from the time when such action could have been instituted, in accordance with the recorded deed.

ART. 135. Mortgages legally created on property which hereafter can not be mortgaged in accordance with this law, shall be governed, during the time they are in force, by the previous legislation.

ART. 136. Records and cancellations of mortgages shall be made in accordance with the regulations established in titles 2 and 4, for records and cancellations in general, without prejudice to the special provisions contained in this title.

ART. 137. Mortgages are voluntary or legal.

SECTION 2.—*Voluntary mortgages.*

ART. 138. Voluntary mortgages are mortgages which are agreed to between parties, or constituted by the will of the owner of the property on which they are created.

ART. 139. Voluntary mortgages may only be created by persons who have the free disposition of their property, or, in case they should not have it, if they are authorized to do so in accordance with the laws.

ART. 140. Persons who, in accordance with the provisions of the preceding Article, are authorized to create voluntary mortgages may do so personally, or through an agent having a special power of attorney to contract this class of obligations, executed before a Notary Public.

ART. 141. A mortgage made by a third person without sufficient power, may be ratified by the owner of the mortgaged property; but this shall only be effectual from the date of the new record, by which the error committed is rectified.

ART. 142. A mortgage created for the security of a future obligation subject to recorded conditions subsequent, shall be effectual against third parties from the date of record, if the obligation is finally contracted or the condition fulfilled.

If the obligation secured is subject to a recorded condition subsequent, the mortgage shall be effectual as to third persons until it appears from the Registry that the condition has been fulfilled.

ART. 143. When the future obligation has been contracted, or the condition subsequent mentioned in the preceding Article is fulfilled, the interested parties must record it by means of a marginal note in the mortgage record, without which requisite the mortgage created can not benefit nor prejudice third persons.

In the same manner they must enter the nonfufillment of the condition or of the obligation.

ART. 144. Any act or agreement between the parties which might modify or destroy the efficacy of a prior mortgage debt, such as payment, compensation, extension of time, a contract or promise not to demand, the novation of the original contract, or a settlement or compromise, shall not be effectual against third persons unless it is entered in the Registry by means of a new record, by a partial or total cancellation, or by a marginal note, according to the particular cases.

ART. 145. The interest on the loan shall not be considered secured with the mortgage in the manner prescribed by Article 114 unless the stipulation and amount of said interest appear in the same record.

ART. 146. In order that voluntary mortgages may be legally created in a valid manner, it is necessary:

1. That they were agreed to or constituted by a public instrument.

2. That the instrument is recorded in the Registry established by this law.

ART. 147. A mortgagee may proceed against the property mortgaged for the payment of the interest due, no matter at what period the principal is to be paid; but if a third person, whom the proceedings could injure, is interested in said property, the sum demanded can not exceed that due and not paid for the interest for the two years last past and the part due for the current year.

ART. 148. Such part of the interest which the creditor can not demand in a foreclosure suit, he may claim in a personal action, being considered with regard thereto if there be general assignment proceedings, as a creditor protected by a public instrument (acreedor escriturario).

ART. 149. Records of voluntary mortgages can only be canceled in the manner prescribed by Article 82. If the persons who should make the cancellation oppose it, it may be decreed by the Court.

ART. 150. When an annuity (censo) encumbered with a mortgage is redeemed, the mortgagee shall have a right to demand of the redeemer that he either pay his debt entirely, including the interest due and to become due, or that he recognize the mortgage on the estate encumbered by the annuity (censo).

ART. 151. In the latter case of the preceding Article, a new record of the mortgage shall be made, which shall clearly express its recognition by the redeemer, which shall be effectual from the date of the previous record.

ART. 152. A mortgage credit may be conveyed or assigned to a third person totally or partially, provided it is effected by means of a public instrument, notice of which is given to the debtor, and that it is recorded in the Registry.

The debtor shall not be bound by said contract to any greater extent than he was by his own.

The assignee shall be subrogated to all the rights of the assignor.

ART. 153. In a mortgage created to guarantee negotiable obligations or deeds to bearer, when the mortgage interest is alienated or assigned, it shall be understood that the latter is transferred together with the obligation or with the deed, it being unnecessary to give notice thereof to the debtor, or to record the transfer in the Registry.

ART. 154. If, in the cases where it is necessary, a notice to the debtor of the assignment of the mortgage debt is omitted, the assignor shall be responsible for any damage which the assignee may suffer in consequence of this omission.

ART. 155. The interests or debts secured by a legal mortgage can not be assigned until the time they are due, and the persons in whose names they stand, have the legal capacity to convey them.

ART. 156. A mortgage shall be effectual with regard to third parties until the record is canceled.

SECTION 3.—*Legal mortgages.*

ART. 157. Only those established in Article 168 are legal mortgages.

ART. 158. The persons in whose favor this law creates legal mortgages shall have no other right to demand the creation of a special mortgage sufficient to secure their interest.

ART. 159. To constitute a legal mortgage it is necessary that the document, by virtue of which it was created, has been recorded.

ART. 160. The persons in whose favor this law establishes legal mortgages may demand the constitution of a special mortgage on any real property or property rights possessed by the person who is obliged to make it, always provided it is mortgageable under this law.

They may also demand this mortgage at any time, even though if the reason on which it was founded has ceased, such as marriage, guardianship, minority, or administration, provided the obligation which was to be secured is not fulfilled.

ART. 161. After a legal mortgage has once been created and recorded it has the same effect as a voluntary mortgage without any other exceptions than those expressly specified in this law, whoever may be the person who is to exercise the rights conferred by said mortgage.

ART. 162. If several estates are offered for the creation of a legal mortgage, and the interested persons do not agree to the amount which is to be secured by each, the Judge or Court shall decide in accordance with Article 119, after a report of experts.

The Judge or Court shall decide in the same manner questions arising among the interested parties as to the sufficiency of the estate offered for the creation of any legal mortgage.

ART. 163. Whenever the recorded legal mortgages become insufficient, the persons who, according to this law, have either the right or obligation to do so, may request the right or must demand the obligation of their sufficiency or amplification.

ART. 164. Recorded legal mortgages shall remain in force until the rights for the security of which they were created have been extinguished, and they shall be canceled in the same manner as voluntary mortgages.

ART. 165. To judicially constitute or amplify any legal mortgage at the instance of a litigant, the procedure shall be in accordance with the following rules:

1. Any person, who has a right to demand it, shall present a petition to the Judge or Court of the domicile of the person compelled to grant it, requesting that the mortgage be constituted, stating the amount for which it should be created, and stating what property may be thus encumbered, or at least indicating the Registry which should contain the record of the property which said person owns.

2. This petition must necessarily be accompanied by the deed or document giving rise to the right to a legal mortgage, and, if possible, a certificate from the Register in which shall be stated all the mortgagable property owned by the defendant.

3. The Judge or Court shall, in view of these papers, order to appear before it all the persons interested in the creation of the mortgage, so that they can agree, if it be possible, as to the manner of constituting it.

4. Should they come to an agreement, the Judge or Court shall order the mortgage created in the manner agreed upon.

5. Should they fail to agree, either as to the obligation to mortgage, or as to the amount which is to be secured, or as to the sufficiency of the mortgage offered, a copy of the petition shall be given the defendant, and the proceedings shall follow the course established for such cases in Articles 732 to 744 of the Law of Civil Procedure in force in the Philippines, and 748 to 760 of that in force in the Antilles.

ART. 166. In cases where the Judge or Court must proceed, by reason of a duty imposed, to demand the constitution of a legal mortgage, he shall order the proper Register to send him the certificate mentioned in Rule No. 2 of the preceding Article; in accordance thereto he shall order the person obligated to constitute the mortgage to appear before him, and with his consent and that of the Department of Public Prosecution he shall continue the proceedings in the manner prescribed.

ART. 167. The provisions contained in the two preceding Articles shall be understood without prejudice to the Regulations established for mortgages given to secure property, which is to be set apart, and the bonds of guardians, and shall not be applicable to a legal mortgage in favor of the State, provinces, or towns, except when the administrative regulations do not establish any other procedure by which they may be demanded.

ART. 168. A legal mortgage shall be made:

1. In favor of married women on the property of their husbands:

For the dowry which may have been formally delivered to them in the presence of a notary;

For gifts which said husbands may have offered them within the limits of the law;

For the personal property, in addition to the dowry, which the wives may have brought with them on their marriage, which, with the same formalities, they may have delivered to their husbands;

For any other property that the wives may have brought on their marriage and delivered to their husbands with the same formalities.

2. In favor of the relatives referred to in Article 811 of the Civil Code, on the property of the person who shall have the duty to do so, for the property which said article declares subject to be set apart; and in favor of the children, on the estates of their parents, for those which the latter must set apart for them according to the law, and for those which belong to said children while they are minors in charge of the father or mother, in case the latter should remarry.

3. In favor of the heirs of the deceased spouse on the property of the surviving one, for the share of the inheritance, the use of which the latter has a right to enjoy according to law, in case specific property passes into his or her possession for this purpose, in case of remarriage.

4. In favor of minors or incapacitated persons on the property of their guardians, for the amount the latter may have received from them and for the responsibility they incur, unless they give a bond for security instead of a mortgage bond.

5. In favor of the State, provinces, or towns, on the property of persons making contracts with them or administering their interests, for the liabilities which they incur in accordance with the law; on the property of taxpayers for the amount of an annual tax thereon, which has fallen due and has not been paid.

6. In favor of underwriters on property insured, for the insurance premiums for two years; and if the insurance is based on the mutual system, for the last two assessments which may have been declared.

DOWRY MORTGAGES.

ART. 169. The married woman in whose favor this law established the legal mortgage shall have a right to demand:

1. That the husband mortgage and record in the Registry in her name, all the real property and property rights which he may have received as appraised dowry or with the obligation of returning their value.

2. That all the other property which the husband receives unappraised and which he must return, in a proper case, be recorded in the Registry, if it has not already been done, as dowry, or personal property in addition to the dowry, or by whatever legal designation it may have.

3. That the husband secure, by means of a special sufficient mortgage, all other property not embraced in the preceding paragraphs, and which is delivered to him by reason of the marriage.

ART. 170. The dowry admitted by the husband, the delivery of which is not certified to or only appears from a private document, shall have no other effect than that of a personal obligation.

ART. 171. Notwithstanding the provisions of the preceding article, a woman who may have a dowry acknowledged in her favor by the husband, before the celebration of the marriage, or within the first year thereafter, may at any time demand that the husband secure it by a mortgage in her favor, provided she legally proves the existence of the dowry property or other similar or equivalent property at the time of alleging her claim.

ART. 172. The real property or property rights which are delivered as an appraised dowry shall be recorded in the Registry of Property in the name of the husband in the same manner as any other acquisition of ownership, stating besides, in the record the amount of the dowry of which said property forms part, the amount at which it was appraised, and the dowry mortgage created thereon, provided the husband does not mortgage other property sufficient to secure the appraised value of the former.

ART. 173. If the woman has recorded in her name the real property which is to constitute the unappraised dowry, or the personal property in addition to the dowry, which she delivers to her husband, the proper character of either property shall be described in the Registry, a marginal note for this purpose being entered on said record of the property.

Should said property not be recorded in the name of the wife, it shall be entered in the usual form, stating in the record whether it is a dowry, or personal property in addition to the dowry.

ART. 174. When on recording appraised dowry property in the name of the husband, the Register is obliged to enter the mortgage in favor of the wife, and the deed which is presented be not sufficient for this purpose, he shall suspend the record and enter the necessary cautionary notice.

ART. 175. The legal mortgage created by the husband in favor of the wife shall guarantee the restitution of the property or its appraised value only in case such restitution takes place in accordance with the laws and with the limitations prescribed therein; and it shall cease to have effect, and may be canceled whenever for any legal cause the husband is exempted from the obligation to restore it.

ART. 176. The sum which must be secured by virtue of an appraised dowry shall in no case exceed the value of its appraisement; and if the value of said dowry is reduced because it exceeds the sum permitted by law, the mortgage shall likewise be reduced in the same proportion, after the proper partial cancellation has been made.

ART. 177. When an unappraised dowry is created on property other than real, it shall be appraised for the sole purpose of fixing the amount that the mortgage is to secure, in case said property does not exist at the time it should be restored, the dowry not losing thereby its character of being unappraised, if it was thus qualified in the dowry deed.

ART. 178. A mortgage to secure gifts by reason of marriage, shall only be made should they be offered by the husband as increasing the dowry. If they are offered without this requisite they shall constitute a personal obligation, the husband having the option of securing them by mortgage or not.

ART. 179. The husband is not obliged to create a mortgage for the personal property in addition to the dowry of his wife, unless the latter is conveyed to him for his administration by a public instrument properly executed before a Notary.

ART. 180. To constitute the mortgage referred to in the preceding Article, the property shall be appraised or its value fixed by those who, according to this law, have a right to demand it and to determine its sufficiency.

ART. 181. Property brought in marriage, for the effects of the last paragraph of number 1 of Article 168, shall be understood to be such property which in any matter whatsoever, in accordance with local customs, the wife brings to the conjugal partnership, provided it is conveyed to the husband by means of a public instrument properly executed before a Notary for his administration, either by appraisement in view of its sale, or with the obligation of keeping it or returning it on the dissolution of the marriage.

When the delivery of the property mentioned in the preceding paragraph appears only by the acknowledgment of the husband, the creation of a dowry mortgage can not be demanded, except in the cases and manner prescribed by Article 171.

ART. 182. A married woman who is of age may herself demand the creation of the mortgage and record of property mentioned in Article 169.

If she has not as yet contracted the marriage, or if she has done so and is a minor, said right shall be exercised in her name and the sufficiency of the mortgage created shall be determined by the father, the mother, or the person who gives the dowry, or the property which should be secured.

ART. 183. In default of the persons mentioned in the preceding article, and the woman being a minor, whether married or single, the extension of these rights must be demanded by the guardian, his substitute, the family council, or any of its members.

ART. 184. If the guardian or his substitute, or the family council do not demand the creation of the mortgage, it shall be the duty of the Public Prosecutor to demand, or at the instance of any person, a demand may be made, to compel the husband to execute the same.

ART. 185. Municipal judges shall also have the obligation of inducing the Department of Public Prosecution to see that the provisions of the preceding Article are complied with.

ART. 186. If the husband does not possess any property with which to create the mortgage mentioned in number 3 of Article 169, he must create it on the first realty or property rights he may acquire; but this obligation can not prejudice a third person until the mortgage is recorded.

ART. 187. When the dowry consists of rents or perpetual annuities, and they are alienated, their restitution shall be secured by creating a mortgage for the principal represented by said rents or annuities capitalized at the legal rate of interest.

ART. 188. If the annuities referred to in the preceding Article are of a temporary character and could or should continue after the dissolution of the marriage, a mortgage shall be created for the amount agreed to between the husband and wife, and, should they not come to an agreement, for the amount fixed by the Judge or Court.

ART. 189. The provisions of this law with regard to dowry mortgages do not alter or modify the provisions contained in Articles 880, 881, and 909 of the Code of Commerce.

MORTGAGES FOR PROPERTY TO BE SET APART.

ART. 190. The special mortgage, which minor children have a right to demand by reason of the property to be set apart, shall be created under the following conditions:

1. The father shall present to the Judge or Court an inventory and appraisement made by experts of the property which is to constitute the security, with a statement of the property which he offers for mortgage, accompanied by the title deeds proving his ownership thereof, and

documents showing its value and its freedom from all incumbrances or specifying what liens exist thereon.

2. If the Judge or Court considers the account of the property correct, and the mortgage offered sufficient, a memorandum shall be issued in the proceedings, declaring what realty is set apart, so that this reservation may be embraced in the proper records of ownership, and shall create the mortgage for the value of the rest of the property subject to be set apart on that under the absolute ownership of the father, which is offered as security.

3. Should the Judge or Court be in doubt as to the sufficiency of the mortgage offered by the father, he may order the latter to take the necessary steps or present the documents which he may deem necessary to prove its sufficiency.

4. Should the mortgage not be sufficient, and should the father have other property on which it can be created, the Judge or Court shall order it to be extended to such property as, in his judgment, is sufficient to secure the rights of the child. Should the father not possess any other property, the Judge or Court shall order it created on the property offered, but shall express in the decree that it is not sufficient and declare the obligation of the father to extend it to the first realty he may acquire.

5. The memorandum mentioned in number 2 of this Article shall contain all the details which a mortgage record should embrace, and shall be signed by the father, certified by the Clerk of the Court, and approved by the Judge or Court.

6. By means of the presentation to the Registry, of a copy of this memorandum, and of the decree of its judicial approval, the proper record and entry shall be made to certify that the property may be set apart to constitute the mortgage mentioned in number 2.

ART. 191. If ninety days elapse and the father has not presented to the Judge or Court, the record of the proceedings mentioned in the preceding Article, the fulfillment thereof may be demanded by relatives, whatever may be their degree, by the executor of the deceased spouse, or in default by the Department of Public Prosecution.

ART. 192. The period of ninety days mentioned in the preceding paragraph shall be computed from the time that the property should be set apart, on account of the contraction of a second or subsequent marriage.

ART. 193. If two or more of the persons mentioned in Article 191, apply for the creation of the legal mortgage, preference shall be given to the one making the first application.

ART. 194. Should the children be of age, only they themselves can demand the creation of the mortgage in their favor.

ART. 195. The Judge or Court which approved the record of proceedings mentioned in Article 190 shall see, under his or its responsibility, that the records and entries prescribed by number 6 of the same Article are duly made.

ART. 196. Should the father not have any mortgageable property, the proceedings provided in Article 190, shall also be instituted for the sole purpose of recording what is set apart and its value.

ART. 197. The decree issued in the case of the preceding Article shall only express what is necessary, regarding what is set apart and its value, and the obligation of the father to mortgage the first realty he may acquire.

If the property set apart consists of realty, the Judge or Court shall order that its classification be entered in the Registry in the manner prescribed by Article 173.

ART. 198. The mother shall give security for the rights of her children to the property set apart, with the same formalities as the father.

ART. 199. The special mortgage to secure the property set apart, established by Article 811 of the Civil Code, may only be demanded by the relatives in whose favor the property is to be set apart, should they be of age. If they are minors, the persons who legally represent them shall demand it in their name. In either case, the interest of the persons in whose favor the property is to be set apart, shall be secured, with the same requisites mentioned in the preceding Articles, including, with regard to the property to be set apart, the provisions relating to the father.

MORTGAGES OF PROPERTY OF PERSONS STILL UNDER PARENTAL AUTHORITY.

ART. 200. The father, or when there is none, the mother, is the legal administrator of the property of the children who are still under his or her authority, although with the obligation of creating a legal mortgage in favor of the latter, should he or she contract a second marriage.

ART. 201. The children in whose favor legal mortgages are established by the preceding Article, shall have a right to demand:

1. That the realty belonging to them be recorded in their name, if this has not already been done.

2. That the father, or, in a proper case, the mother, secure by a special mortgage, if it can be done, the property other than realty, belonging to the said children.

ART. 202. It shall be understood that the father, or, in a proper case, the mother, can not create the mortgages mentioned in the preceding Article, should they not have any mortgageable real property.

ART. 203. If the real property which the parents possess is insufficient, they shall, however, create a mortgage thereon, without prejudice to its extension to other property which they may subsequently acquire, should they be required to do so.

ART. 204. The extension of the rights mentioned in Article 201 may be demanded in the name of the children by:

1. The persons from whom the property is derived.

2. The heirs or executors of said persons.

3. The ascendents of the minor.

ART. 205. Neither the father, or, in a proper case, the mother, can convey the real property belonging to the child, of which they enjoy the use or administration; nor can they encumber it, except for justified reasons of profit or necessity, and with the previous authority of the Judge of the District, on hearing the Department of Public Prosecution.

ART. 206. In case the persons mentioned in Article 204 do not demand that the rights expressed in Article 201 be accorded, the Public Prosecutor may do so by reason of his duty.

MORTGAGES BY REASON OF GUARDIANSHIP.

ART. 207. The guardian, before his charge is conveyed to him, and to insure a good result from his administration, shall give a bond, which must be either a mortgage or a bond for security.

ART. 208. The mortgage bond shall be entered in the Registry of Property.

ART. 209. Pending the execution of the bond, the substitute of the guardian shall exercise all the administrative acts, which the family council may consider indispensable for the preservation of the property, and to collect the income therefrom.

ART. 210. The record of the mortgage bond, when such bonds are given, must be demanded by:

1. The guardian.
2. The substitute of the guardian.
3. Any member of the family council.

ART. 211. The persons omitting the formalities mentioned in the preceding article shall be responsible for any loss or damage.

ART. 212. A mortgage bond must secure:

1. The value of the personal property which comes into the hands of the guardian.
2. The rents or income which the property of the minor or incapacitated person yields during the period of one year.
3. The profit which the minor may receive during one year from any mercantile or industrial enterprise.

ART. 213. The family council is charged with the duty of fixing the amount of the mortgage bond and its determination.

ART. 214. A mortgage bond may be increased or reduced during the exercise of the guardianship, according to the changes in the value of the property of the minor or incapacitated person.

ART. 215. A mortgage bond can not be totally canceled until after the accounts of the guardianship have been approved, and the guardian has satisfied all the responsibilities of his administration.

ART. 216. The following are exempted from giving security as guardians:

1. The father, the mother, and the grandparents in case they are called upon to assume the guardianship of their descendants.

2. The testamentary guardian relieved from this obligation by the father, or, in a proper case, by the mother. This exemption shall cease when subsequently to his appointment, reasons arise unknown by the testator, which should make the giving of a bond indispensable, in the opinion of the family council.

3. A guardian appointed and exempted from giving bond by strangers, who may have made the minor or incapacitated person their heir or left them an important legacy. In this case the exemption shall be confined to the property or income of which the inheritance or legacy consists.

OF OTHER LEGAL MORTGAGES.

ART. 217. The competent official shall require the creation of special mortgages on the property of persons administering public funds or who have made contracts with the State, provinces, or towns, in all the cases, and in the manner prescribed by the administrative regulations.

ART. 218. The State, province, or towns shall be preferred to any other creditor in the recovery of one year's taxes on the realty.

To secure a like preference for a larger sum than that represented by said taxes, the State may require a special mortgage, in the form prescribed by the administrative regulations.

ART. 219. The person insuring real property shall have a right to require a special mortgage on the property insured, the owner of which has not satisfied the insurance premiums for two or more years, or two or more of the last assessments, if the insurance is based on the mutual system.

ART. 220. While the premiums for the last two years, or, in a proper case, the last two assessments are not paid, the claim of the insurer shall have preference over any other claims.

ART. 221. When the two assessments or premiums referred to in the two preceding Articles are due and have not been satisfied, a mortgage shall be created for the whole sum that is due, and the entry thereof shall be effectual only from its date.

TITLE VI.

OF THE MANNER OF KEEPING THE REGISTRIES.

ART. 222. The registry of property shall be kept in books folioed and rubricated by the Judges of First Instance of a subdistrict, or by the Municipal Judges delegate for the inspection of Registries.

ART. 223. The books mentioned in the preceding Article shall be uniform for all Registries, and shall be formed under the direction of the Colonial Department, with all precautions necessary for the prevention of any fraud or forgery which might be committed therein.

ART. 224. The only books valid shall be those made by the Registers, in accordance with the provisions of the preceding Article.

ART. 225. The books of the Registry can for no reason whatsoever be removed from the office of the Register. All judicial or extrajudicial proceedings requiring the exhibition of said books shall be held in the office itself.

ART. 226. The books shall be numbered in their chronological order.

ART. 227. The Registry of property shall embrace records or entry cautionary notices, cancellations, and notes of all documents subject to record according to Articles 2 and 5.

ART. 228. The Registry of property shall be kept by opening a special record for each estate in the proper book, entering as the first record thereof the first one which is demanded with relation to said property, provided it refers to transfer of property.

When the first entry that is demanded is not of this kind, the last record of ownership which may have been made in the old books shall be transferred to the new ones, in favor of the owner of the property encumbered by the new record. All subsequent records, entries, and cancellations shall be made immediately following each other, without leaving any blank space between them.

ART. 229. The entries relating to each estate shall be numbered in their proper order and signed by the Register.

ART. 230. One book shall be opened for each municipal district wholly or partially included within the jurisdiction of a Register.

ART. 231. The books of each municipal district shall have a special numeration in proper order, besides that mentioned in Article 226.

ART. 232. The Government may order, for reasons of public convenience, that a municipal district be subdivided into two or more sections, and that a Registry book be opened for each one of them.

ART. 233. In the case mentioned in the preceding article, to the numeration which the books must have, according to Articles 226 and 231, shall be added the words "Section First" or "Section Second," or the proper one.

ART. 234. When a deed embraces several real properties or property rights located within one municipal district, the first entry made shall contain all the details prescribed by Article 9, and in the following ones the estate only shall be described, should it be necessary, or the property right which is the subject of each of them shall be described, and the nature of the instrument or contract shall be stated, the names of the grantor and of the grantee, the date and town where the instrument was executed, and the name of the Notary who authenticated it, or of the official who executed it, making reference for all other details to said first record, stating the liber and folio containing it.

ART. 235. If the instrument referred to in the preceding Article is one creating a mortgage, the record must express, besides the details prescribed in said Article, the part of the debt for which each estate or interest is liable.

Art. 236. If the property or interests contained in one deed, are located in two or more municipal districts, the provisions contained in the two preceding articles shall be applied to each of said districts.

If any of the latter have been divided into sections, in accordance with the provisions of Article 232, each section shall be considered as if it were a municipal district.

Art. 237. The Register shall authenticate, with his signature in full, the entries of presentation contained in the Day Book, as well as the records, cautionary notices and cancellations, and the notes, with an abbreviation of his name.

Art. 238. Registers shall also keep a book called a Day Book, in which they shall make a brief entry of the contents of every document at the time of its presentation.

Art. 239. The entries in the Day Book shall be numbered in proper order at the time of their inscription.

Art. 240. The entries mentioned in the preceding Article shall be made in the order in which the documents are presented, without leaving any blank space between them, and shall contain:

1. The name, surname, and residence of the person presenting the document.

2. The hour of its presentation.

3. The character of the document presented, its date, and the official or notary subscribing it.

4. The character of the interest created, conveyed, modified, or abrogated by the document to be recorded.

5. The nature of the estate or property right which is the subject of the document presented, with a statement of its location, its name, and its number, should it have any.

6. The name and surname of the person in whose favor the record is desired.

7. The signature of the Register and of the person who presents the document, or of a witness, should that person not be able to sign.

Art. 241. When the Register makes the record, cautionary notice, or cancellation to which the entry of presentation refers, in the proper book, he shall state this fact by means of a marginal note opposite said entry of presentation, stating the volume and folio where the former may be found, as well as the number of the estate according to the Registry and the number given to the requested record.

Art. 242. Every day not a working day, at the time previously indicated at which the Registry is to be closed in the manner prescribed by the Regulations, the Day Book shall be closed by a memorandum executed by the Register, immediately after the last entry he may have made. Mention shall be made therein of the number of entries executed during the day, or if none have been made, this fact shall also be stated.

If the time for closing the Registry should arrive before an entry is terminated, it shall be continued until its conclusion, but without, however, admitting any other document in the meantime and stating this circumstance in the final memorandum.

19539——4

ART. 243. Entries of presentation made after the office hours of the Registry shall be null.

ART. 244. At the foot of any document recorded in the Registry of property, the Register shall affix a note, signed by himself, expressing the kind of entry which has been made, the liber and folio containing it, the number of the estate, and the number of the record made.

ART. 245. No entry shall be made in the Registry of property until the fees established or to be established by law are previously paid, should any be due for the instrument or contract to be recorded.

ART. 246. Notwithstanding the provisions of the preceding Article, the entry of presentation may be made before the payment of the fees; but, in such case, the entry shall be suspended and the document shall be returned to the person who presented it, so that, after its examination. he may liquidate and satisfy said fees.

When these have been paid the interested person shall return the document to the Registry, and the record shall be made, the effects of which shall retroact to the date of the entry of presentation, provided the deed has been returned within the thirty days immediately following the date of said entry.

If the deed is returned after said thirty days have elapsed, a new entry of presentation shall be required, and the effects of the entry made shall retroact to the date of the new entry. In case the fees have not been paid because the office or official having in charge their liquidation or collection, has consulted with his superiors as to some doubtful question regarding the case, the period of thirty days shall be suspended from the time of said consultation, until the matter is definitely settled, which circumstance shall be stated in a marginal note opposite the entry of presentation, the document which the interested party must present to the Register being seen by the latter, provided this officer is not certain as to the fact.

ART 247. The liquidation of the fees which must be paid in each case shall be made through the proper office or official in the manner prescribed by the Regulations.

ART. 248. Receipts for fees collected for instruments and contracts subject to record, shall be made in duplicate, and both copies shall be delivered to the person making the payment. One of these copies shall be presented to the Register, who shall file it in his office.

The Register who should not preserve said copy shall be directly liable to the Treasury for the fees which may not have been liquidated.

ART. 249. In order that any entry may be made in the Registry by virtue of a judicial decree, the Judge or Court shall issue the proper order in duplicate.

The Register shall return one of the copies to the same Judge or Court from whom it was received, or to the interested party who may have presented it, with a note signed by him, stating that it has been complied with, and keeping the other one in his office, making thereon a

51

rubricated memorandum similar to the one made on the copy returned. The documents shall be filed in one package, numbered in the order of their presentation.

ART. 250. To totally or partially cancel a mortgage, the document by virtue of which it is to be made shall be presented, as well as the instrument creating it, which shows that it has been recorded. On both documents a memorandum shall be made stating that the cancellation and its entry have been executed in accordance with Article 244.

In order that the persons interested in the cancellations may not be deprived of the document, when it is a public instrument, a copy on common paper shall be presented therewith, signed by said persons. After being compared by the Register he shall state its conformity with the original, by means of a memorandum, filing it and returning the original to the interested person.

Registers shall preserve in their chronological order in numbered packages the documents by virtue of which any mortgage is canceled.

ART. 251. Any other documents which may be presented to the Register, shall be returned to the interested parties with the memorandum mentioned in Article 244 affixed thereto, after the proper use thereof has been made.

ART. 252. The persons interested in a record, cautionary notice, or cancellation may demand that before the principal entry thereof is made in the book a draft of said entry be shown them.

Should they note any error or important omission they may demand its correction, applying to the President of the Audiencia or to his representative, should the Register refuse to comply.

The President of the Audiencia or his representative shall decide what is necessary, without any formal proceedings and within the period of six days.

ART. 253. Whenever the interested person has had notice of the draft in the manner prescribed in the preceding Article, and he expresses his satisfaction therewith, or, in default thereof, the President of the Audiencia should decide the form in which it should be made, either circumstance shall be mentioned in the proper entry.

TITLE VII.

OF THE CORRECTION OF ENTRIES IN REGISTRIES.

ART. 254. Registers may themselves correct, on their own responsibility, any material errors committed—

1. In the entries of principal records, cautionary notices, or cancellations, the respective documents being on file in the office.

2. In entries of presentation, marginal notes, and notes of references, although the documents are not on file in the office of the registry, provided the respective principal record is sufficient to show the error, and that it is possible to correct it in accordance therewith.

Art. 255. Registers can not correct material errors committed without the consent of the interested party possessing the recorded document, or in default thereof, without a judicial decree, in the following cases:

1. In records, cautionary notices, or cancellations, the documents of which are not on file in the office of the Registry.

2. In entries of presentation and notes, when said errors can not be proved by the respective principal records, and the documents are not on file in the office of the Registry.

Art. 256. Errors of judgment committed in entries, records, or cancellations, or in any other entries referring thereto, when they do not clearly appear from the same, shall not be corrected without the unanimous consent of all the interested parties and of the Register, or without a judicial decree ordering it.

The same errors committed in entries of presentation and notes may be corrected by the Register himself, when the respective principal record suffices to expose them.

Art. 257. The Register, or any of the persons interested in an entry, may oppose the correction which another person requests on account of an error of judgment, provided that in his opinion the judgment considered incorrect be in accordance with the deed to which the entry refers.

The question arising in this connection shall be decided by a declaratory suit.

Art. 258. When the errors, material or of judgment, produce the nullity of the record, in accordance with Article 30, they can not be corrected, and the nullity thereof shall be demanded and declared by the proper Court in the suit instituted for this purpose.

Art. 259. A material error shall be considered committed for the purpose of the preceding Articles, when some words are unintentionally written for others, when the statement of some detail is omitted not causing its nullity, or when mistakes are made as to surnames or amounts in transcribing them from the documents, without thereby changing the general sense of the record or any of its parts.

Art. 260. An error of judgment shall be considered committed when, in expressing in the entry matters contained in the deed, their sense is altered or varied, this error not necessarily producing nullity in accordance with the provisions of Article 30.

Art. 261. Material errors which are committed in the writing of entries can not be remedied by means of corrections, scratches or erasures, nor by any other means except by a new entry, in which the error committed in the first one shall be clearly stated and corrected.

Art. 262. Errors in judgment shall be corrected by means of a new entry, which shall be executed by the presentation of the document already recorded if the Register acknowledges his error or if the Judge or Court declares it; and by virtue of a new document if the error is caused by the vague, ambiguous, or incorrect language of the original deed, and the parties agree thereto, or it is so ordered by a judicial decree.

ART. 263. Whenever a correction is necessary on account of an error of any kind committed by the Register, and it can be made by virtue of the same document previously presented, all the expense and damages caused shall be defrayed by the Register who committed the error. Should the one who committed said error not be the same one making the correction, the latter may demand of the former the payment of the corresponding fees, according to the schedule in force, for the new record and other work.

If to make the correction a new document is necessary all expenses shall be defrayed by the persons interested.

ART. 264. The corrected part shall only be effectual from the date of its correction, without prejudice to possible rights of third persons to institute proceedings on account of the falsity or nullity of the document to which the entry refers, which contained the error of judgment, or an account of the entry itself.

TITLE VIII.

ADMINISTRATION AND INSPECTION OF REGISTRIES.

ART. 265. Registries of property shall be under the jurisdiction of the Colonial Department, and their affairs, as well as those of the Notaries, Civil and Marriage registry, and Mercantile registry, shall be in charge of the Registry and Notarial Division established by this law.

ART. 266. The personnel of the Division mentioned in the preceding Article shall consist of one chief, at an annual salary of 10,000 pesetas; two clerks, one first. at 8,700, and one second, at 7,500; three assistants, one first, at 6,000 pesetas, one second, at 5,000, and one third. at 4,000.

Said Division shall also have four copyists: Two first, at an annual salary of 2,000 pesetas, and two second, at 1,500.

Vacancies in the positions of chief, clerks, and assistants shall be filled strictly by promotion, in accordance with the grades previously established, and those of the lowest assistants by competitive examination. The vacancies in the positions of copyists shall be filled in the same manner. The Government may, reserving the privileges which this paragraph provides, in case of vacancies, for the good of the service and with the consent of the full Council of State, abolish one or more of the positions in the Division; the persons filling the same to receive two-thirds of the salary they were receiving until they are reinstated with the same salary and privileges.

ART. 267. The officials of the Division can not be removed by the Government without just cause, with reference to the fulfillment of the duties of their positions. by virtue of proceedings instituted for this purpose and after consulting the corresponding Division of the Council of State. An opportunity must be given the interested party to make an explanation in writing regarding the matter which gave rise to the proceedings.

ART. 268. It shall be the duty of the Registry and Notarial Division:

1. To transact, directly with the Colonial Minister and through the Chief of said Division, all business within its jurisdiction, and to propose the measures necessary to consolidate the Registries of Property in the colonies and for the faithful observance of this law and of the regulations which may be enacted for its execution.

2. To execute such papers as may be prepared to fill vacant Registries, and for the holding of competitive examinations, when they are necessary, as well as those for the discharge of employees of the Division, or of Registers making the final disposition necessary in each case in accordance with the law.

3. To decide administrative appeals on the determination of documents made by Registers and the doubts which arise in the minds of said officials regarding the interpretation and execution of this law or of the regulations, provided they do not require dispositions of a general character which must be made by the Secretary of the Colonies.

4. To form and publish statements relating to transfers of property, in accordance with the data received from the Registers.

5. To exercise a general inspection and supervision of all the Registries in the Colonies, through the Presidents of the proper Audiencias, and even through Judges of First Instance, or Municipal Judges delegated to the inspection of Registries, and through the Registers themselves, when it is deemed advisable for the good of the service.

The other duties of the Division shall be determined by the Regulations.

ART. 269. The Presidents of Audiencias shall be inspectors of the Registries within their jurisdiction and shall immediately exercise such functions through the Judges of First Instance of the respective subdistricts, or, where this is not practicable, through the Municipal Judges, who may be delegated for this purpose.

In towns where there is more than one Court of First Instance the Judge designated by the President of the Audiencia shall exercise the functions mentioned.

ART. 270. The President of the Audiencia or his delegates shall inspect the Registries the last day of each quarter, making a memorandum of the condition in which they were found.

The Presidents of Audiencias may, besides the quarterly inspection, personally or through their delegates make any extraordinary inspection they may deem advisable, either to inspect the whole Registry or only certain of its books.

For the extraordinary inspections the Presidents of Audiencias may delegate their functions, if they deem it necessary, to an Associate Justice of the Audiencia or to a Judge of First Instance, when the usual delegate is a Municipal Judge.

ART. 271. The delegates shall transmit to the Presidents of Audiencias the statements mentioned in the first paragraph of Article 270 within three days following the termination of their inspection.

ART. 272. The Presidents of Audiencias shall transmit to the Colonial Department every six months a detailed report of the condition of the Registries which are subject to their inspection and authority.

ART. 273. Should the Presidents of Audiencias note any lack of formalities on the part of the Registers in the conduct of the Registries, or any infraction of the law or of the regulations for their execution, they shall take the steps requisite for their correction, and, in a proper case, punish them in accordance with the provisions of the same law.

If the error or infraction could be qualified as a crime, the culprit shall be placed at the disposal of the Courts.

ART. 274. Should the President of an Audiencia find that a Register has not furnished bond, or has not deposited a quarter of his fees in accordance with the provisions of Article 305, he shall immediately suspend him.

ART. 275. Should the President of an Audiencia suspend any Register he shall appoint another to temporarily fill the office, and shall give a report showing the reasons of his action to the Colonial Department.

ART. 276. Registers shall consult directly with the President of an Audiencia, or with the Judge of First Instance, concerning any doubt they may entertain as to the interpretation and execution of this law, or of the regulations which may be enacted for its application.

Should the Judge of First Instance entertain any doubt as to the decision of the question, he shall forward it, together with his report, to the President of the Audiencia.

Should the President of the Audiencia also be in doubt as to the decision of the question submitted by the Judge of First Instance or by the Register, he shall forward it to the Colonial Department.

ART. 277. Whenever the doubt which gave rise to the question of the Register prevents the entry of some principal record in the Registry of Property, a cautionary notice shall be made thereof, which shall have all the effects mentioned in the ninth paragraph of Article 42.

The decision of the question, in such case, shall be transmitted directly to the Register within the sixty days provided in paragraph 96 for the duration of said entries.

Should said decision not be transmitted within the sixty days, the notice shall continue its effect.

ART. 278. No fee shall be charged to the interested party for entering the cautionary notice mentioned in the preceding Article.

TITLE IX.

PUBLICITY OF REGISTRIES.

ART. 279. Registries shall be open to those who are known to have any interest in ascertaining the status of the real property or property rights entered or recorded.

ART. 280. Registers shall exhibit the books in a convenient place for persons who may wish to consult them, without taking them from the office and with the precautions necessary to insure their preservation.

ART. 281. Registers shall issue certificates:

1. Of entries of all kinds contained in the Registry relating to property indicated by the persons interested.

2. Of certain records which the said persons may indicate, either specifying them or referring to those of one kind or another which may exist in relation to certain property.

3. Of mortgage records and cancellations thereof made at the instance or in favor of said persons.

4. Of the non-existence of a record of any kind or of a particular kind, relating to specified property or in charge of certain persons.

ART. 282. The certificates mentioned in the preceding Article may refer to a fixed and stated period, or to everything that may have been filed since the original establishment of the said Registry.

ART. 283. The freedom or encumbrance of real property or property rights can only be proven to the prejudice of third persons by the certificates mentioned in the foregoing Article.

ART. 284. When the certificates mentioned in Article 281 are not in conformity with the records to which they refer, the latter shall be preferred, reserving the action which the person prejudiced thereby may bring to recover the proper indemnity from the Register who committed the error.

ART. 285. Registers shall not issue the certificates mentioned in the preceding Articles, except at the written request of the person who may have any interest in ascertaining the status of the realty or of the property right in question, or by virtue of a judicial order.

ART. 286. Should the Register refuse to exhibit the books or to give certificates of entries contained therein, the person who requested it may appeal to the President of the Audiencia, if he resides in the same place, or to the person delegated for the inspection of the Registry. The President of the Audiencia or his delegate shall decide after hearing the Register. If the decision is rendered by the delegate, an appeal lies to the President of the Audiencia.

ART. 287. The petitions of the interested parties and the mandates of the Judges or Courts, by virtue of which the Registers are compelled to issue certificates, must very clearly express:

1. The character of certificate demanded in accordance with Article 281, and if it is to be a literal one or an abstract.

2. The information, according to the character of such certificate, sufficient to indicate to the Register the property of persons in question.

3. The period to which the certificate should be limited.

ART. 288. Certificates shall be given of the entries in the Registry of property.

They shall be given of the entries in the Day Book also, if at the time of their issue there be any awaiting inscription in said Registry, which should be embraced in the certificate requested, and if it is a question of proving that some estate is free of encumbrances or that some interest does not in fact exist.

ART. 289. Registers shall not issue certificates of entries in the Day Book unless the Judge or Court so order, or unless it is expressly requested by the interested parties.

ART. 290. Certificates shall be literal or abstract, according as they may be ordered or requested.

Literal certificates shall consist of the respective records in full.

Certificates in abstract shall state all the circumstances contained in said records which are necessary for their validity, according to Article 30, as well as the incumbrances which at the time are a lien on the realty or recorded interest, according to the proper entry, and any other point which the interested party may designate or which is considered important by the Register.

ART. 291. Registers, after examining the books, shall issue their certificates only regarding the property, persons, or periods designated in the petition or mandate, without making reference to any other entries or details than the ones demanded, with the exceptions contained in the second paragraph of Article 288 and in Article 292, but, nevertheless, without omitting any which may be considered embraced in the terms of said mandate or request.

ART. 292. When a certificate of any given record is demanded or ordered, either literal or abstract, and the entry indicated has been canceled, the Register shall make a literal copy of the entry by virtue of which the cancellation took place.

ART. 293. When a certificate of encumbrances on realty is requested, and no encumbrance appears in the Registry in force at the time or made by the person designated, the Register shall state this fact.

If any encumbrance does exist, he shall copy it literally or in abstract, in accordance with the provisions of Article 290, and shall then add that no other encumbrance appears to be in force.

ART. 294. Should the Register be in doubt as to whether some record is in force, being doubtful also as to the validity or efficiency of the cancellation referring thereto, he shall copy both entries in the certificate, verbatim, whatever may be the form of the latter, stating that this was done in view of a doubt as to whether said cancellation had all the conditions necessary to produce its legal effects, and also his reasons for the doubt.

ART. 295. Registers shall issue the certificate demanded of them, in the shortest possible time, but never exceeding four days for each estate, records, or condition of the estate whether free or encumbered, which are to be certified to.

ART. 296. After the period mentioned in the preceding Article has elapsed, the interested persons may apply to the President of the Audiencia or to his delegate requesting that the delay be justified and proceeding in accordance with the provisions of Article 286.

TITLE X.

APPOINTMENT, QUALIFICATIONS, AND DUTIES OF REGISTERS.

ART. 297. Every Registry of property shall be in charge of a Register.

Registers of property shall be considered public officers for all legal effects and shall be addressed as "Excellency."

They may be retired with pension at their own request on account of physical disability, duly proven, or after reaching the age of sixty-five years. After reaching the age of seventy years said retirement with pension shall be compulsory. In their classification the time they have filled the office of Register and eight years more by virtue of their profession shall be taken into account. As the regulating salary, in the absence of a higher one, for the determination of a pension, in the declaration of pensions for old age, widowhood, and orphanage, there shall be assigned those designated to Chiefs of Administration of the third class for Registers of the first class, and to Chiefs of Bureaus of the first and second classes for the Registers of the second and third classes, respectively.

The Secretary, after a report from the Registry and Notarial Division, may grant leaves of absence for a period not to exceed five years to the Registers who may request it. The first vacancy which occurs in their class at the expiration of their leave shall be filled by any Register whose leave of absence has expired, and in case he should not accept the position he shall be definitely dropped from the Corps.

The officials of the Registry and Notarial Division having been placed on the same basis as Registers of property for the purposes of Rules 1 and 2 of Article 303, the provisions of the two foregoing paragraphs shall also apply to them; it being understood that in cases of leaves of absence they shall still be kept on the rolls of the Division as supernumeraries, being promoted as if they were rendering active service, and at the expiration of their leave, occupying the first vacancy in the class they belong to, according to said rolls.

They shall also be considered as on leave should they be elected Deputies or Senators during their term of office and with the privileges allowed them in case their positions are abolished according to Article 266.

Any Register who resigns without just cause or who is removed in accordance with the provisions of Article 308, shall have no right to the privileges mentioned in the third paragraph of this Article.

Registers who cease to perform their duties because of the change or abolition of the Registry, and who are not immediately placed in another of the same or of a higher class, shall be considered as on leave of absence, and may be classified as a "cesante" (dismissed for political or economical reasons, but continuing to draw a salary), giving him credit for the time he had charge of the Registry. If, according to the time computed, he should be entitled to pay or to a temporary pension (cesantía) in accordance with the regulations governing retired classes, he shall receive the salary corresponding to his years of service and the regulating salary which he may have received or the one previously stated. If the Register on leave is appointed to another Registry of the same or of a higher class and he resigns without cause, he shall lose the time credited to him by virtue of his service in this profession, and shall therefore not receive the salary or increase of temporary pension thereof which he would have had a right to in consequence of this time.

Registers can not exchange their positions except with other Registers of the same or of the next lower class, and only when a good reason exists therefor in the judgment of the Government.

To ascend a class by exchange it is indispensable to have served in the next lower one four years or to have entered it by means of a competitive examination.

ART. 298. To be appointed Register it is necessary:

1. To be a Spaniard and a layman.
2. To be over twenty-five years of age.
3. To be a lawyer.

ART. 299. The following can not be appointed Registers:

1. Insolvents or bankrupts who have not yet received their discharge.
2. Debtors to the State or to public funds as taxpayers or in the settlement of their accounts.
3. Persons accused of crime, pending their trial.
4. Persons sentenced to correctional or punitive penalties, until they obtain their rehabilitation.

Registers who come under case 3 of this Article can not take part in the competitive examinations mentioned in rule No. 1 of Article 303.

ART. 300. The office of Register shall be incompatible with that of Senator, Deputy to the Cortes, Provincial Deputy, Municipal Judge, or Assessor, when acting in the capacity of Judge of First Instance, Mayor, or Member of a Municipal Council, Notary, and with any office or employment which carries with it similar jurisdiction, or is paid from State, Provincial, or Municipal Funds.

ART. 301. Each Registry shall have such clerks and assistants as the Register shall need, appoint, and pay, who shall discharge the duties assigned them by the Register, but under his sole and exclusive responsibility.

ART. 302. Registers shall be appointed by the Colonial Department.

ART. 303. Vacancies in the office of Registers of property which occur in the Colonies shall be filled in accordance with the following rules:

1. Every three vacancies occurring shall be filled by Colonial and Peninsular Registers; the first shall be filled by the Register of the highest class, and the senior one in service from among the candidates; the second by the Register who among the candidates is the senior, without regard to class; the third by the Register of a higher, equal, or the next lower class to the Registry which is to be filled, whom the Government selects, taking into consideration the qualifications of the candidates. No Register can, in competition with others having legal conditions, receive two promotions as to class in order of merit, without two years elapsing between each promotion, unless he renders a new important service well known to be worthy of immediate reward.

2. If there be no Registers of the classes mentioned in the preceding paragraphs, the vacancy may be filled by any person selected by the Government, taking into account their qualifications.

3. Registers of property who have been disciplined and deprived of promotion can in no case attain a higher class nor even be transferred to another of the same class during the time of the duration of their punishment.

4. Registries which are vacant, and have been announced in their proper order and are not desired by licensed Registers, shall be filled by means of competitive examinations, two places for these examinations being established, one in the capital of Cuba, Puerto Rico, or the Philippines, in whichever of these islands the vacancy has occurred, and another in the capital of Spain.

ART. 304. Persons who have been appointed Registers can not take possession of their office without previously giving bond, the amount of which shall be fixed by the Regulations.

ART. 305. If the person who has been appointed Register does not give the bond mentioned in the preceding paragraph, he must deposit in the official establishment authorized by law to receive such deposits a quarter of his fees until the amount of the bond required is deposited.

ART. 306. The deposit or, in a proper case, the bond mentioned in the preceding Article shall not be returned to the Register until three years after he has ceased to discharge his duties, during which time the Judge of First Instance of the proper subdistrict shall make the announcement in the official papers of the respective colony, and in the "Gaceta de Madrid," so that it shall reach all persons who may have some action they may wish to bring against said Register.

ART. 307. The bond of Registers and, in a proper case, the deposit shall be subject, until it is restored, to the liabilities incurred by them by virtue of their office, which shall have preference over any other obligations of said Registers.

ART. 308. Registers can not be removed nor transferred to other Registries against their will, except by virtue of a judicial order. or by the Government in accordance with proceedings instituted by the President of the Audiencia, after hearing the interested party and a report from the Judge of First Instance of the subdistrict.

To permit the removal or transfer by the Government the proceedings must show that some wrong has been committed by the Register in the fulfillment of his duties, or which lowers him in the eyes of the public, and the proper Division of the Council of State shall also be heard.

ART. 309. As soon as Registers take possession of their office they shall propose to the President of the Audiencia the appointment of a substitute to take their place during their absence or illness, having the right to select for this position either one of the officials of the Registry or any other person in whom they have confidence.

If the President of the Audiencia is satisfied with the person proposed he shall immediately appoint the substitute. Should he be not satisfied, because of some serious reason, he shall order the Register to propose some other person.

The substitute shall discharge his duties under the responsibility of the Register, and shall be removed at any time the latter may request it.

ART. 310. Registers shall at the end of each year make six detailed statements:

The first, of alienation of realty made during the year, their liquidated prices, and the fees paid on them into the Public Treasury.

The second, of rights of use, use and occupancy, servitude, annuities (censos), or any other property rights in realty, with the exception of mortgages, their value in principal and income, and the fees paid on them into the Public Treasury.

The third, of mortgages created, number of estates mortgaged, amount of the principal secured thereby, the cancellations of mortgages which have taken place, number of estates released, amount of capital returned, and fees paid into the Public Treasury.

The fourth, of loans, notwithstanding that they have been embraced in the preceding statement by reason of being mortgage loans, their number, amount of principal loaned, and interest stipulated and fees paid into the Public Treasury.

The fifth, of the estates the ownership or possession of which has been recorded in the Registry for the first time, their value, if it appears, and their superficial area.

The sixth, of the number of documents presented, old and new, proceedings instituted, certificates issued, and fees received for all the services rendered.

The regulations shall contain the other requirements which said statements must contain, and the manner of drafting them.

ART. 311. Registers shall transmit the statements mentioned in the preceding Article to the Presidents of Audiencias before the 1st day of April, who shall forward them to the Colonial Department before the 1st day of June, with such remarks as they may deem proper.

ART. 312. Registers shall receive the fees which are established by this law, and shall pay the expenses of keeping and conducting the Registries.

TITLE XI.

RESPONSIBILITY OF REGISTERS.

ART. 313. Registers shall be civilly liable, in the first place, on their bonds, and in the second place, with their property, for all loss or dam-· age they may cause:

1. By not recording in the Day Book, or not entering or making a cautionary notice within the time fixed by the law of the documents presented to the Registry.

2. For any error or inaccuracy committed in records, cancellations, cautionary notices, or marginal notes.

3. For canceling without good reason any entry record or omitting the entry of any marginal note within the proper time.

4. For canceling any record, cautionary notice, or marginal note without the document and the requisites demanded by this law.

5. For any error or omission in the certificates of records or freedom from incumbrances of realty or of property rights, or for not issuing said certificates within the time fixed by this law.

ART. 314. Errors, inaccuracies, or omissions indicated in the preceding Article can not be chargeable to the Register when they are due to some defect in the recorded document itself, and provided they are not of those which are manifestly and according to Article 19, number 9 of Article 42, and Articles 100 and 101, would have caused the denial or suspension of the record, entry, or cancellation.

ART. 315. The correction of errors committed in entries of any kind, which are not due to others committed in the respective deeds, shall not free the Register from the liability which he may incur for the damage that may have been caused by said errors before they were corrected.

ART. 316. The Register shall be liable on his bond and with his property for indemnities and fines which may arise through the acts of his substitute during the time the latter has charge of the Registry.

ART. 317. The person who, by error, malice, or carelessness of the Register, should lose a property right or the action to recover it, may immediately demand that the Register refund the value of what he has lost.

The person who, for the same reasons, loses only the mortgage of an obligation, may either demand of the Register that he create a mort· gage equal to the one lost, or that he immediately deposit the amount, thus securing said obligation when it falls due.

ART. 318. The person who, through error, malice, or carelessness of the Register, is released from some recorded obligation, shall be jointly responsible with the Register for the payment of the indemnity for which the latter may be liable by reason of his error.

ART. 319. Whenever in the case of the preceding Article the Register indemnifies the person damaged, he may bring an action to recover the amount paid against the person who, through his error, was released from the recorded obligation.

When the person damaged brings his action against the person benefited by said error, he can not proceed against the Register unless he does not obtain the indemnity sued for, or obtains only a part thereof.

ART. 320. The civil action which, in accordance with Article 317, the person damaged brings on account of the errors of the Register shall not prevent or arrest a penal action, which in a proper case may be instituted in accordance with the laws.

ART. 321. Any action which may be brought against the Register for the purpose of holding him liable shall be commenced and heard before the Inferior Court having jurisdiction of the Registry District in which the error has been committed.

ART. 322. Infractions of this law, or of the regulations for its execution, committed by Registers, although not causing any damage to third persons nor constituting a crime, shall be punished without the formality of a trial, by the Presidents of Audiencias, by the imposition of fines of 50 to 500 pesos.

ART. 323. Final judgments awarding damages and sentencing Registers to indemnify loss or damage shall be published in the Gaceta de Madrid and in the official papers of the proper Colony, if they are to be enforced against the bond, because the person condemned has not paid the amount of the indemnity.

By virtue of this publication, the persons who believe themselves damaged by other acts of the same Register may bring their actions, and should they not do so within the period of one hundred and twenty days the judgment shall be carried out.

ART. 324. If any actions are brought within one hundred and twenty days, the execution of the judgment shall be suspended until other final judgments in their favor are issued, unless it is manifest that the bond is sufficient to pay the amount of said claims after the judgment has been carried out.

ART. 325. Should the bond not be sufficient to pay all the claims which are considered good, its amount shall be divided pro rata among the persons who presented them.

The provisions of the preceding paragraph shall be understood to be without prejudice to the liability of the rest of the property of the Register.

ART. 326. The President of the Audiencia shall immediately suspend the Register ordered by a final judgment to pay the loss and damages, if within ten days he does not do so or make good his bond, or if he does not secure the claimants for the amount of their respective suits.

ART. 327. The person injured by the acts of a Register who does not file his claim within the period of one hundred and twenty days mentioned in Article 323 shall be indemnified with what remains of the bond of the Register, or with his property, and without prejudice to the provisions of Article 318.

ART. 328. If the claim for indemnity has been admitted and the amount of the bond does not appear sufficient to secure it, the Judge or Court must, at the instance of the claimant, order that a cautionary notice be made against the property of the Register.

ART. 329. Should the Register be condemned at the same time to pay damages and losses, and also to pay fines, the former shall be first paid.

ART. 330. The period for the restitution of bonds must be computed from the time the interested party ceases to exercise the office of Register and not from the time he leaves one Registry and is transferred to another.

ART. 331. When a Register who passes from one Registry which requires a larger bond to another requiring a smaller one, the difference shall not be returned to him except at the time and under the conditions prescribed in Article 306.

ART. 332. The right of action to recover indemnity for the damage and loss suffered by the acts of Registers shall be limited to one year after said losses have been known to the person who may bring said action, and in no case shall it last a longer period than that indicated by the common law for the limitation of personal actions, computed from the time the offense was committed.

ART. 333. The Judge or Court before whom a Register is prosecuted for the indemnity of damages caused by his acts shall immediately advise of the action the President of the Audiencia under whose jurisdiction said Register is.

The President of the Audiencia, in view thereof, shall require the Judge or Court to order the entry of the cautionary notice mentioned in Article 328, should it be deemed necessary and should it not have already been ordered; requesting at the same time that he be informed at certain intervals as to the progress of the action.

The person who during one hundred and twenty days does not prosecute the claim he has filed shall be understood to have renounced his right.

TITLE XII.

FEES OF REGISTERS.

ART. 334. Registers shall collect the fees for the entries they may make in the books, and for the certificates they issue, in strict accordance with the Schedule accompanying this law.

Acts and work for which no fees are stipulated in said Schedule shall not be entitled to any compensation.

ART. 335. The fees of the Register shall be paid by the person or persons in whose favor the record or entry of the interest is directly made.

ART. 336. When there are several persons involved in the transaction the Register may demand payment from any of them, and the person making it shall have the right to recover from the others the part he may have paid on their account.

In any case the fees may be recovered judicially, but the entry shall never be refused or suspended on account of nonpayment.

ART. 337. Entries made in the indices and in any of the auxiliary books kept by Registers shall not be charged for.

ART. 338. In the fees mentioned in the Schedule for the certificates of Registers the price of the stamped paper on which they have to be executed is not included and shall be paid for by the persons interested.

ART. 339. At the foot of every entry, certificate, or note for which fees have been charged the Register shall stamp the amount charged, quoting the number of the Schedule by virtue of which it was demanded.

When one number of the Schedule is applied to several operations it shall be sufficient to record the fees charged at the foot of the principal entry or note, quoting the corresponding number of the Schedule, it being unnecessary to record in the other work the fees embraced in said number.

ART. 340. The fees charged by Registers for certificates and records ordered by Judges or Courts in consequence of actions in which they have jurisdiction shall be classified for their exaction and collection in the same manner as the other costs of said action.

ART. 341. When a Judge or Court decides that the refusal of a Register to definitely record or enter a document is unfounded, the person interested shall not be obliged to pay the fees for the cautionary notice, or, in a proper case, for the marginal note which said Register may have placed opposite the entry of presentation at the time the document was returned, nor for the cancellation of said note.

ART. 342. When an entry is corrected on account of some error committed therein by the Register, the latter shall not receive any fee for the new entry, but without prejudice to the provisions of the second paragraph of Article 263.

If the Register who made the mistake in the entry is not the same who is to make the correction, the latter shall have a right to bring an action against the former or his heirs for the recovery of the fees due for the new record.

ART. 343. For records, certificates, and other work, for which fees may be collected, incumbent upon Registers, these officials shall charge the fees indicated in the respective numbers of the Schedule, taking into account the value of the estates, or the interest created in them, which are transferred, or to which the operations indicated refer.

ART. 344. Registers, in writing the entries, notes, and certificates, shall act strictly in accordance with the instructions and models which the regulation for the execution of this law will contain.

Art. 345. The delegates of the Presidents of Audiencias for the inspection of Registries shall carefully examine in their visits of inspection to see if the records are made in conformity with the models indicated in the preceding Article, and they shall state in their report any errors of this kind they may observe, so that the Register who makes his entries more extensive than necessary or omits therein some of the details which they should contain, according to their class, may be disciplined.

Art. 346. No changes whatsoever may be made in the Schedule accompanying this law except by the enactment of another law.

Title XIII.

REDEMPTION FROM EXISTING ENCUMBRANCES.

Art. 347. Persons who may have any realty or property rights recorded in their favor may release them with regard to third persons:

1. From any legal mortgages or interests which have not been recorded to which they are or may be subject.

2. From charges which may not have been recorded or secured by a recorded mortgage, caused by a suit to establish or rescind an instrument, which can have no effect with regard to third persons without being recorded.

3. From the interests which, if having been recorded in the books kept by the old Recorders and Judges who received mortgages, the Register in whose charge said books are has not been able to determine the property which is affected thereby, the entries being defective.

4. From all suits to establish or rescind an instrument which can be brought, including those of the persons who may have previously recorded their titles relative to the same property or interests.

Art. 348. If, on the day this law is put into operation, the persons requesting the release have the ownership of the realty or property rights recorded in the books of the old "Anotaduría" or "Receptoría" of mortgages their request can not be complied with until they transfer the entries to the new books of the Registry.

Art. 349. For the effects of No. 1 of Article 347 shall be considered as not recorded besides the interests which are not entered in the old nor in the new books, those which have not been recorded in favor of any person nor been the object of judicial proceedings during the thirty years prior to the time this law has been put into operation, and were not entered in favor of their present owners before said period.

Art. 350. Interests considered not recorded, in accordance with the preceding Article, may be the basis of proceedings to clear the title.

Art. 351. The Judge of First Instance of the district in which the property or real interests are situated to which said proceedings refer is the only one who may declare it.

ART. 352. If the proceedings to clear the title of an estate situated in two or more districts is demanded, the Judge of competent jurisdiction shall be the one of the district in which is located the principal part thereof, such part being considered the one which contains the residence of the owner, or if there be none, the workrooms, and if there be no workrooms the part having the greatest area.

ART. 353. If the property to which the proceedings to clear the title refer be a railway, canal, or other work of a similar nature, or having a resemblance thereto, which crosses several districts, the principal part shall be considered such part, for the effects of the preceding Article, in which is situated the place from which the work starts.

ART. 354. In the proceedings for redemption may also be included, in the manner prescribed by Article 347, general mortgages established in accordance with prior legislation which are in force when this law is put into operation, viz:

1. In favor of married women, on the property of their husbands, for the dowry and personal property in addition to the dowry which has been delivered to them.

2. In favor also of married women, on the property of their husbands, for the dowry and donations by reason of marriage settlements which the latter may have made to them.

3. In favor of children, on the property of their parents, for the property which may be set apart.

4. In favor of children who are still under parental authority, on the property of their parents, for the property of which the latter are administering or enjoying the use.

The persons in whose favor these general mortgages stand can not demand the creation of a special mortgage.

ART. 355. The mortgages mentioned in the preceding Article, which are in existence on the day this law is put into operation, shall continue in force in accordance with prior legislation, for the time the obligations which they secure hold good, with the following exceptions:

1. When, by the consent of the parties or of the debtor, they are replaced by special mortgages.

2. When the married woman or children, being of age, consent to the extinguishment, reduction, subrogation, or extension of the legal mortgage.

3. When legal mortgages have no further effect with regard to third persons, by virtue of a decree issued in the suit for clearing the title, as established in this title.

ART. 356. Persons who, on the day this law is put into operation, may have their property encumbered by some implied mortgage, as mentioned in Article 54, may at any time demand of the person holding said mortgage that he accept in its place a sufficient special and definite mortgage.

Should said person refuse to accept the mortgage offered, or should he accept it and the persons interested do not agree as to the amount of the obligation to be secured, or as to the insufficiency of the property offered in security, the Judge or Court shall decide the matter in the manner prescribed by Article 165.

ART. 357. The provisions contained in the preceding Articles do not alter or modify the preference allowed by law in the property other than realty or property rights therein, to those persons in whose favor legal mortgages have been created.

ART. 358. Registers of property have charge of the preparation or proceedings for clearing title.

ART. 359. A single proceeding for clearing title may be instituted for all the property comprised in the jurisdiction of the Registry, provided said jurisdiction embraces one subdistrict.

ART. 360. If the jurisdiction of a Registry comprises two or more subdistricts one proceeding shall be instituted for each subdistrict in which is situated the property which it is desired to clear.

ART. 361. The practice of proceedings for clearing title shall be in accordance with the following rules:

1. The interested person shall present to the proper Register a petition for each proceeding instituted.

2. In the petition shall be described the property or property rights the clearing of which is requested, with a statement of the encumbrances thereon and which are to remain in force, notwithstanding the clearing of the title, the legal mortgages and unrecorded interests, as well as all actions to establish or rescind title which may be brought against the property, if there be any and they be known; the names of the persons interested in said mortgages, interests, and actions, and their domiciles, if they be known; the names of the wife and children of the petitioner, should he have any, giving their age, status (whether married or single), and domicile, and the names of the persons who, during the twenty years immediately preceding, may have owned, according to the Registry, said property or interests; and the petition shall be made that one hundred and eighty days be fixed, either to request the creation of a special mortgage to replace the general one or to exercise the rights and actions which the persons referred to, or any others, may have, with a warning that, should they not be brought within said period the said legal mortgages, rights, or actions mentioned shall be considered as extinguished with regard to third persons who may subsequently acquire the ownership or a property right in any of the property cleared.

3. The Register shall certify at the end of this document as to the conformity of its contents with the entries in his books, should they so conform, or as to any differences which may exist.

Should the differences be material, he shall return the document to the interested party for its correction, or so that he may make use of his privilege.

Should the differences be immaterial, or should those it did contain have been corrected, the Register shall consent to the proceedings asked for in the petition to clear title, and shall make a report to the Judge of First Instance of the proper subdistrict.

4. In case the clearing of an estate located within the jurisdiction of several Registries is requested, the Register who institutes the proceedings shall notify those of the other jurisdictions, so that they may issue the certificate prescribed in the preceding rule, each one for the part of the estate which corresponds to his office, for which purpose the former shall transmit a complete copy of such part of the petition as may be necessary.

5. The following shall be notified personally or by means of a notice in accordance with the provisions of Articles 246, 247, 250, 251, 252, and 253 of the Law of Civil Procedure of the Philippines; 262, 263, 266, 267, 268, and 269 of the same law for Cuba and Puerto Rico:

First. The wife and children of the petitioner, should he have any, and, if they be minors, their guardians, or in the absence of such, the representative of the Department of Public Prosecution.

Second. The persons, if there be any, or their legitimate representatives, who appear from the document clearing the title or from the Registry, interested in any legal mortgages, rights, or actions which should be extinguished on clearing the title.

Third. The persons, if they exist, who during the last twenty years may have had, according to the Registry, the ownership of the property or interests which it is desired to clear.

6. In notifying each person interested of the request of the petitioner, a notice shall be delivered to each, signed by the Register, stating:

First. The name, surname, domicile, status (whether married or single), and profession of the petitioner;

Second. The property described in the petition for clearing the title;

Third. A designation of the part of the property which he desires to clear, should it not be the entire property;

Fourth. The kind of legal mortgage, interest, or action in which the person notified may be interested, and

Fifth. The period of one hundred and eighty days allowed in which to bring an action and the Court before which the suit must be instituted.

7. The notices shall be made by said Register in accordance with the above-mentioned Articles of the Law of Civil Procedure, if the persons notified reside in the same town where the Register is located.

Should they reside outside of said town, but within the jurisdiction of the Registry, the Register shall send a communication to the proper Municipal Judge, so that he may order the Secretary to make said notification. Should they reside outside of the jurisdiction referred to, the Register shall communicate the fact to the Judge of First Instance of the subdistrict, so that the latter may issue the necessary letters requisitorial.

8. When the estate which it is desired to clear is mortgaged in favor of the Public Treasury, the notification shall be sent to the Governor of the proper Province, or to the high official having jurisdiction of the matter which served as a basis for the mortgage.

9. Notifications to other persons who may be interested shall be made by means of a proclamation, posted in the usual places in the town where the Registry is established and where the property to which the clearing of title refers is located, said edicts being also published in the official papers of the respective colony.

The proclamations prescribed in the preceding paragraphs shall state:

First. The name, surname, residence, status (whether married or single), and the profession of the petitioner.

Second. A statement of the estates which the latter desires to clear, indicating their location, name, number, area, and boundaries, the deed referring to their last acquisition, and the name of their former owner.

Third. The encumbrances on said property and the ones which are to remain in force notwithstanding the clearing of title.

Fourth. Legal mortgages, interests, or actions to which they are or could be subject, according to the petition of the claimant, and which are to be extinguished by the clearing, should no objections be made.

Fifth. The period of one hundred and eighty days in which to file the claims in the Court of First Instance to which the Registry corresponds, with the proper notice.

10. The period of one hundred and eighty days shall be computed from the date of the official papers in which the proclamation is published, provided all the notifications prescribed in rules 7 and 8 have been made prior thereto. Should they not have been made, the one hundred and eighty days shall be computed from the last notification made, for all interested persons who wish to file some objection.

11. During the period of one hundred and eighty days the proceeding for clearing the title shall be on view in the office of the Register instituting it, so that all persons interested may examine it.

12. After the period of said one hundred and eighty days, the proceedings and all the papers showing the notices and the posting of the proclamations, together with a copy of the official papers in which the latter were published, shall be transmitted by the Register to the proper Judge of First Instance of the subdistrict.

ART. 362. Any objections which may have been presented to said Court of First Instance of the subdistrict, in consequence of the petition for clearing the title, shall not be heard until the Register transmits the proceedings, in accordance with the provisions of the preceding rule.

ART. 363. Before hearing the objections mentioned in the preceding Article, matters regarding declarations of poverty may be heard, and such as refer to the issue of copies or certificates of public documents, which are to serve as a basis for said objections, and any others which, in the judgment of the Judge of First Instance of the subdistrict, are considered urgent.

ART. 364. Should a person request the creation of a special mortgage, a copy of the request shall be given the petitioner, proceeding in the manner prescribed by Article 165.

ART. 365. If more than one person should request such mortgages, all the objections shall be heard in one trial and, until a final decision is rendered thereon, no property shall be declared cleared.

ART. 366. If any rights and actions have been brought which affect all of the property which it is desired to clear, they shall be heard together at one trial.

ART. 367. The provisions of the foregoing Article shall only be made use of when the hearing at one trial is compatible with the nature and object of the claims.

ART. 368. In case the actions brought only affect certain estates, they shall be heard separately.

ART. 369. The procedure in the trials instituted in consequence of the objections referred to in the two preceding Articles, shall be such as are respectively prescribed by the law of Civil Procedure.

ART. 370. If no claim has been filed against the property to be cleared, or the persons who have a right to demand the creation of a special mortgage forego it, with regard to said property, or the actions brought against all of the property in question have been ended, or if a part thereof is not affected by the objections filed, the Judge of First Instance of the subdistrict shall transmit the proceedings for clearing the title to the Department of Public Prosecution to ascertain whether said proceedings have been instituted in accordance with the formalities prescribed by this law, and to determine the property or interests which are to be cleared.

ART. 371. Should the Department of Public Prosecution find any inaccuracies, they shall be ordered corrected, as well as those which the Court should deem necessary to correct, and, after being confirmed, the judgment clearing the title shall be entered.

ART. 372. The judgment clearing the title shall state:

1. The name, surname, number, area, boundaries, and ownership of each of the estates cleared.

2. Whether it has been issued after the trial of other suits or not, mentioning such suits.

3. The fact of having created any special mortgage or mortgages for the security of interests which were previously guaranteed by legal mortgages or unrecorded incumbrances, or that said mortgages were not created on account of the renouncement of the interested parties, or because they have not been claimed, or because none existed.

4. The incumbrances remaining on the property, notwithstanding the clearing.

5. The fact that said estates are entirely free from all unrecorded incumbrances or legal mortgages, with regard to third persons who may later acquire the ownership or a property right in the same property.

The judgment shall be made public in the manner prescribed in the first paragraph of rule No. 9 of Article 361.

ART. 373. In the ten days following the publication of the proclamation in the official papers of the proper colony, an appeal may be taken from the judgment clearing the title to the Audiencia of the jurisdiction, by persons who may have been injured thereby, and who prove that by force majeure, or for other reasons, it was impossible for them to file their claim within the one hundred and eighty days mentioned in rule 10, of said Article 361.

The proper remedy by cassation may be had from the decision of the Audiencia.

Should no appeal be taken within ten days, or if the appeal taken is finally disposed of, confirming the judgment clearing the title, no appeal may be taken from the latter to the prejudice of third persons.

ART. 374. The Judge of First Instance of the subdistrict shall order that a certified copy of the judgment be issued and delivered to the person interested, so that he can present it to the proper Registry, and that the papers in the case be filed.

If an estate has been cleared which is situated in the jurisdiction of several Registries, a certified copy shall be delivered for each of them, confined to the property situated therein.

ART. 375. The Register to whom the certified copy of the judgment is presented shall make a note thereof in the special Registries for estates or interests cleared, stating briefly the contents of said judgment, so far as it refers to each estate. After this has been done, the certified copy shall be filed in the Registry.

ART. 376. In judgments clearing the title the intervention of attorneys or solicitors shall not be necessary.

The stamped paper employed shall be such as is designated by law.

Registers may demand, for the certificate prescribed in rule 3 of Article 361, the fees fixed in the Schedule accompanying this law; for the notifications which they make and, for the posting of proclamations, fees which Clerks of Courts of First Instance receive for the same work, according to the schedule in force for judicial matters, and for the entries of judgments in the special Registries of property, 50 cents for each entry.

In the Courts of First Instance the fees charged shall be in accordance with the schedule mentioned.

ART. 377. Persons who may have the ownership only of realty or property rights recorded, may clear them, in accordance with the provisions of the preceding Articles, with the following modifications:

1. In the petition requesting the clearing of the title, in the notices which are to be delivered to the persons to be notified, and in the

edicts shall be stated the date of the entries or the dates of the entries of ownership.

2. The period of one hundred and eighty days mentioned in Article 361 shall be extended to one year.

3. Notice of the petition for clearing the title must necessarily be given to the Mayor of the town located in the district where the property, which it is desired to clear, is located.

ART. 378. Persons, who neither have the ownership nor the possession of the realty or the property rights recorded, and wish to record said ownership, in accordance with the formalities mentioned in Articles 395 *et seq.*, may request their clearing in the same proceedings, which must be instituted before the Court of First Instance of the subdistrict in which the property is located, provided the instrument, the notices which have to be issued to those interested, and the edicts, contain all the details prescribed in said Articles, and in Article 361.

The Judge of First Instance of the subdistrict shall also proceed in accordance with the provisions of said Articles and Article 362 *et seq.* up to 273, inclusive, with such changes as may be indispensable for the different cases.

ART. 379. The records of ownership which are made by virtue of the judgments entered, in accordance with the proceedings referred to in the foregoing Article, shall contain a statement to the effect that the property is cleared, with a brief statement of that part of the judgment which relates thereto.

ART. 380. Persons who have recorded neither the ownership nor the possession of the realty or property rights, and desire to record only the possession, can not request the judgment clearing the title to said property, or interests, until they have obtained such record, proceeding in this case in accordance with the provisions of Article 377.

ART. 381. Property acquired through inheritance or legacy, can not be cleared until five years have elapsed from the date of their record in the Registry.

ART. 382. Exceptions to the rule contained in the preceding Article are the property acquired by legal heirs.

ART. 383. Persons who on the day this law is put into operation have several estates of their ownership encumbered by an annuity (censo), or voluntary mortgage, the principal of which has not yet been distributed among them, shall have a right to demand that it be divided among those sufficient to secure said principal three times over, in accordance with the provisions of Article 119.

If one of the estates should be sufficient to secure said sum, it can also be demanded that the lien be reduced to the same.

If two or more of the estates in question must remain encumbered, each one must be sufficient to secure three times over that part of the principal which it guarantees.

ART. 384. The creditor or owner of the annuity (censualista), may also demand the division and reduction of the encumbrance in the case mentioned in the preceding Article, should the debtor or the person paying the annuity (censatario) not do so.

ART. 385. If the estates charged with annuities (acensuados), or mortgaged in the manner described in Article 383, should not be sufficient to secure three times over the principal of the annuity (censo) or the debt, the division of said principal can be demanded only among said estates, in proportion to their respective value, but not the clearing of any of them.

ART. 386. The division and reduction of the annuities (censos) and mortgages, mentioned in the preceding Articles, shall be made by mutual agreement between all persons who may be interested in the continuance of either.

Should the parties interested not come to an agreement, or if any one of them is an unidentified person, said division and reduction shall be decreed by the Court in a declaratory suit and with the intervention of the Department of Public Prosecution, should there be any unidentified or unknown interested persons.

ART. 387. If the division or reduction of the annuity (censo) or mortgage is agreed to by all the persons interested, it must appear by means of a public instrument.

Should a suit have been instituted and a judgment rendered, the Court shall issue the proper mandate.

The annuities (censos) which have not been imposed on specified estates, but which have been secured by a general mortgage of all the property of the persons who created them, shall be understood as embraced in this Article, as well as in those following Article 383; therefore, the owner of the annuity (censualista) may demand that a lien for the annuity be created on property indicated, which is the possession of the person paying the annuity, should the latter not do so voluntarily.

ART. 388. Through the presentation of the document, or in a proper case, of the judicial mandate, the new mortgage or lien shall be recorded in the Registry according to the manner in which it has been created, and the previous ones which are to be replaced thereby shall be canceled, should they have been recorded.

TITLE XIV.

UNRECORDED DOCUMENTS AND RECORDS OF POSSESSION.

ART. 389. From the time this law goes into operation, no document or instrument which has not been recorded in the Registry shall be admitted in the ordinary or special Courts or Tribunals, in the Councils or offices of the Government, by which interests subject to record are created, conveyed, acknowledged, modified, or extinguished, according to the same law, if the object of the presentation be to enforce, to the prejudice of third persons, the interests which should have been recorded.

Notwithstanding the provisions of the preceding Article, the document which has not been recorded, but which should have been, may be admitted to the prejudice of third persons, if the object of the presentation be only to corroborate another subsequent instrument which had been recorded.

This document may also be admitted, if it is presented to demand a declaration of nullity and consequent cancellation of some entry which prevents the record of said document.

ART. 390. To facilitate the compliance of the preceding Article, to owners who lack a recorded title of ownership, no matter at what period the acquisition took place, they shall be permitted to record their interest by previously proving their possession, before the Judge of First Instance of the place where the estates are located, with the consent of the Department of Public Prosecution and citation of the adjacent property owners, should they desire to record the absolute ownership of some estate, and with the citation of the owner or other participants in the ownership, should they desire to record some property right.

If the estates are located in a town or township where no Judge of First Instance of the subdistrict resides, said proceedings may be held before the proper Municipal Judge, with the consent of the representative of the Public Prosecutor.

The intervention of the Department of Public Prosecution shall be limited to seeing that the formalities of law are observed in the proceedings.

ART. 391. In the preparation of the papers to which the preceding Article refers, the following rules shall be observed:

First. The document in which the admission of the proceedings is requested shall contain:

1. The nature, location, area, boundaries, name, and incumbrances on the estate, the possession of which it is desired to prove.

2. The legal nature, value, conditions, and incumbrances on the property right, the possession of which is in question, and the nature, location, boundaries, and name, should it have any, of the estate on which such right exists.

3. The name and surnames of the person from whom the realty or interest was acquired.

4. The length of time the possession has been had. The circumstance of demanding a written title or the difficulty of finding it, should it exist.

Second. The proceedings shall be held in the presence of two or more witnesses, landowners of the town or municipal district in which the estates are located.

Third. The witnesses shall prove that they have the qualifications mentioned in the preceding rule, presenting the document necessary for this purpose.

They shall limit their testimony to the statement that the person who instituted the proceedings possesses the estates in his own name, and to the time of said possession, and they shall be responsible for any damage they may cause by the inaccuracy of their depositions.

Fourth. The person who desires to have his possession recorded, shall present a certificate of the Mayor or official intrusted with the collection of land taxes in the town of the municipal district in which the estates are located. This certificate shall clearly set forth, in accordance with the assessment roll, sworn statements or documents presented by the taxpayers, or other data from municipal offices, that the person interested pays the taxes as the owner of the property, stating the amount paid on each estate, if it appears, and should this not be possible, it shall be stated that all of them were taken into account at the time of the last assessment.

When no quarterly payment of taxes has been made because the acquisition has been recent, the person from whom the realty was acquired shall be notified of the proceedings, or his heirs, so that they may declare whether they have any objections to make against its record.

If the person requesting it is an heir of the previous possessor, he shall present the last receipt for the taxes which may have been paid, or any other document showing that the payment was made.

Fifth. If the owners of the contiguous estates, or the part owner of the property or interests in an estate, who must be cited, are absent, and their whereabouts are known, the Court shall cite them by means of a communication, if they reside in the colonies, or he shall address himself through the Colonial Department, if the persons are to be found in the Peninsula, or in any of the other colonies. If their residence be in some foreign country, the communication shall be addressed through the same official channels to the consul of the country in which they are residing, requesting them to appear in person or by proxy within the period deemed convenient, according to the distance, and which can not be less than ninety days, computed from the date of the notice.

If their whereabouts are unknown, they shall be cited by means of official edict published in the official papers of the proper Colony, and within the period of ninety days; and, if at the end of this period the persons cited should not appear, the Court shall approve the proceedings and order that the record of the interest be made without prejudice to the interests of said contiguous owners or part owners, and stating that the latter have not been heard in the proceedings.

The record shall in such case also contain said statement.

Sixth. Any person, who believes that he has a right to the estates or a part thereof, the record of which is requested through an information as to possession, may institute a declaratory suit to enforce it before the Court of competent jurisdiction.

The interposition of this claim and its entry in the Registry shall suspend the course of the proceedings with regard to the information, or the entry thereof, should they already have been concluded and approved.

ART. 392. Should the notice drawn in accordance with the form prescribed in the preceding Article, be sufficient, and there be no opposition by a person having a right thereto, or such a position as was made, having been abandoned, the Court shall approve the proceedings, and order that the record requested be made in the Registry without prejudice to a third person having a better claim.

The possessor who may have acquired the decree mentioned in the preceding paragraph, shall present to the Registry, in requesting the proper record, the original papers in the case which have been turned over to him for this purpose, being permitted to transmit therewith a copy of the same on common paper, should he desire to keep them, which, after being compared by the Register and the certificate of comparison attached thereto, shall be returned to him, the original in all cases being filed.

ART. 393. Registers, before recording any estate or interest by virtue of the notices prescribed in the three foregoing Articles, shall carefully examine the Registry to ascertain whether it contains any entry relating to the said realty, which may be totally or partially canceled in consequence of said record.

Should he find any record of acquisition of ownership or possession not canceled, and which is in contravention to the fact of possession justified by the judicial information, he shall suspend the record, enter a cautionary notice, if requested to do so by the person interested, and shall transmit a copy thereof to the Court which approved said information.

The Judge, thereupon and on the citation and consent of the persons who, according to said record, may have some interest in the realty, shall confirm or revoke the decree of approval, in either case communicating the decision rendered to the Register so that he may either make the record or cancel the cautionary notice.

If the persons who should be cited are absent, the formalities prescribed by rule No. 5 of Article 391 shall first be complied with.

Should the Register find uncanceled any record of an annuity (censo), mortgage, or any property right in the estate which should be recorded, he shall make the entry of possession requested by virtue of judicial information, but he must state therein the existence of such record.

Entries of possession shall be converted into records of ownership when they have the following requisites:

1. That twenty years have elapsed since the date of entry.

2. That the conversion of the entry of possession be announced by means of a proclamation in the proper Official Bulletin, so that persons interested, who consider themselves prejudiced thereby, may object by bringing the proper action within the period of thirty days; and

3. That after the periods mentioned in the preceding paragraphs having elapsed, no entry or note exists in the Registry indicating that the prescription has been interrupted.

For this purpose, if the interruption be a natural one, it shall be proven in a summary procedure before the Judge of the Municipality where the property is located, the cause thereof, and how the possession ceased on that account for more than one year; and the certified copy having been issued, the proper note shall be made at the margin of the entry of possession. If the possession has been civilly interrupted, it shall be so stated in the Registry, either by means of a marginal note made by virtue of a communication from the Court, in which the citation of the person possessing the property shall be copied, or by reason of the presentation of a certified copy of the agreement, either by means of a cautionary notice of the claim, the effects of which shall retroact to the date of the presentation to the Registry of the copy of said agreement, or by the record of the instrument which contains the express or implied acknowledgment of the right of the owner by the person in possession. Thirty days after the twenty years have elapsed the Registers shall, at the instance of the persons interested, make the proper record of conversion, if the requisites mentioned in the preceding paragraph have been complied with.

ART. 394. Records of possession shall contain all the details mentioned in Article 391, and also the names of the witnesses who may have testified, the result of their depositions, the result of other investigations made in the proceedings, the opinion of the Department of Public Prosecution, and the special circumstances of the record, according to its character, so far as they appear from the papers in the case.

If the twenty years calculated from the date of the entry have not elapsed, or the requisites mentioned in Article 393 of this law have not been complied with, the entries of possession shall have the legal effect embraced in the provisions contained in the following paragraphs.

The period of possession which appears to have elapsed at the time said entries are made shall be computed for the prescription which does not require a just title, unless a person prejudiced thereby denies it, in which case said period of possession must be proven in accordance with the common law.

Entries of possession shall prejudice or favor third persons from the date of their record, but only with regard to the effects which the laws attribute to mere possession.

The entry of possession shall not prejudice the person who has a better right to the ownership of the realty, although his title has not been recorded, unless the prescription has confirmed and secured the claim recorded. Between the parties the possession shall be effectual from the date prescribed by the common law.

The provisions contained in the preceding Articles, regarding the entries of possession, can not be applied to mortgage rights, which can not be recorded unless an instrument in writing is presented.

ART. 395. Any person in possession, who should not have a written title of ownership, without regard to the period the acquisition took place, may record said ownership by complying with the following formalities:

1. He shall present to the Judge of First Instance of the subdistrict in which the estates are located, or to the one in whose district the principal part thereof is located, if it is an estate situated in various subdistricts, explaining the manner in which he acquired them, and the legal proofs which he can offer of said acquisition, and requesting that, with the citation of the person from whom said property was acquired or his legal representative, and of the Department of Public Prosecution, the proofs mentioned be admitted and his right declared.

2. The Judge shall give a copy of this document to the Department of Public Prosecution, shall cite the person from whom the property was acquired or his legal representative, should he be known, and the persons who have any property right in said property; he shall admit all the pertinent proofs which may be offered by the claimant, by the interested persons cited, or by the Department of Public Prosecution, within the period of one hundred and eighty days, and he shall issue a call for the unknown persons whom the desired record might prejudice, by means of proclamations posted in public places, and which shall be published three times in the official papers of the proper colony, so that they may appear, if they desire to substantiate their claim.

If the persons to be cited should be absent, the procedure established for citations in rule number 5 of Article 391 shall be pursued.

3. After said period has elapsed, the Judge shall take cognizance of the claims and proofs submitted, in writing, to the Department of Public Prosecution, or to others taking part in the suit, and in view of their allegations, and deciding on said proofs with an impartial judgment, he shall declare whether the ownership of the property in question is proven or not.

4. The Department of Public Prosecution, or any of the persons interested, may appeal from this decision, and, should they do so, the appeal shall be conducted in the manner prescribed for proceedings in the nature of a demurrer by the Law of Civil Procedure.

5. If said decision is agreed to or confirmed, it shall be sufficient title for the record of the ownership.

6 When the value of the realty does not exceed 1,000 pesos, the proceedings which, according to rule 3, must be submitted in writing to the Department of Public Prosecution and to the persons interested, shall be oral; and the appeal, should one be taken, shall be in accordance with the procedure established for these appeals in actions for small amounts.

ART. 396. The person in possession of a property right to some estate, the owner of which should not have recorded said ownership when this law is put into operation, may request the record of his interest in the manner prescribed by the regulations. as well as a cautionary notice of the interest of the owner, in accordance with number

9 of Article 42, until the owner of the realty, on being cited, comes forward to contradict the entry or to record his property within the period of thirty days.

The owner of the encumbered estate can not impugn this entry unless he requests at the same time a record of ownership, presenting the proper deed or proof of having commenced proceedings disputing title and demanding the judicial declaration of said ownership.

Should the owner of the realty be absent, the formalities provided for citations in rule number 5 of Article 391 shall first be complied with, and the time shall be computed from the date of the notice.

TITLE XV.

EFFECTS OF ENTRIES CONTAINED IN THE OLD BOOKS AND OF THE RESTORATION OF THOSE RENDERED USELESS BY FIRE OR OTHER ACCIDENTS.

ART. 397. The entries contained in the Registries existing in the offices of "Contadurías," "Anotadurías," or "Receptorías" of mortgages shall have their proper effect, in accordance with the law in force before the mortgage law was put into operation in the respective colonies, if said entries have been or are transferred to the new books of the Registry.

Records of annuities (censos), mortgages, liens or any other property right contained in said books existing in the offices of the Contadurías, Anotadurías, or Receptorías of mortgages must be transferred to the books of the new Registry within the period of one year from the time of the promulgation of this law. This transfer must be made at the request of an interested party.

If the transfer is solicited through a request addressed to the Register within said period, the effects of the transfer shall retroact to the date of the entry in the old books, this fact being stated in the new ones. If the request is filed at a subsequent date it can not prejudice third persons.

If the encumbered estates should not be recorded either in the old or in the new Registry, the record of ownership or possession must first be made in the manner prescribed by the present laws in force, at the instance of the person who has the property right in question recorded in his name.

If the person who requests the transfer is not the same one in whose favor the lien is recorded, he may have it recorded in his name, either by presenting the deeds of ownership proving his right, or by proving that he is actually in possession thereof, by any of the means indicated in Title XIV of this law; but the person, or his legal representatives, who, according to the Registry, appears to have an interest in the lien, must always be cited, either personally or through a proclamation.

If, in transferring the records referred to in the present Article, some of their details are taken from additional notes presented by the interested parties, the part of the new records referring to said details, shall not prejudice third persons.

In case the details presented refer to the boundaries of an agricultural estate, that part of the record relating thereto shall prejudice the owners of the contiguous land who may have signed it.

Owners of annuities (censos), incumbrances, and other interests who request the transfer of the records contained in the old Registries, within the time fixed by this Article, shall be exempted from the payment of the fees, fines, and charges for delay in the proceedings which took place before said period had elapsed, and for the entry made in their favor, and they shall pay the Registers only half the usual fees, it being understood that in the new Registry not more than one entry shall be made for each incumbrance of property right, which shall include the old one, the conveyances which took place thereafter, and the interest of the person in possession.

Records contained in the books of the Registry, prior to said date, shall have all the effects of entries subsequent thereto with regard to the interests they set forth, although the former may lack some of the details which, under penalty of nullity, are required by Articles 9 and 13 of this law, and although they are not transferred to the new books.

ART. 398. If, on account of some accidental or intentional destruction, the books of the Registry of property are totally or partially destroyed, the judicial authority usually delegated to inspect the Registries, shall without loss of time make an extraordinary inspection with the assistance of the Register or his substitute, and, in the absence of both, with the Department of Public Prosecution, and the report thereof shall contain as clearly as possible the condition of the Registry, stating the books or parts thereof which have been destroyed and the measures provisionally adopted to attend to the public service.

When the inspection has been made, the said official shall, as soon as possible, transmit to the Colonial Minister a copy of said report through the President of the Audiencia.

ART. 399. Instruments which can not be definitely recorded on account of the loss or destruction of the books of the Registry, shall be entered as a cautionary notice, in accordance with number 8 of Article 42.

The entry made for this reason shall cease to be effectual after the termination of the period mentioned in the following Article, if the instruments proving the acquisition of the estate or right have not been entered before this law is put into operation.

ART. 400. The records, entries, marginal notes, and other memoranda contained in the books of the old offices of the Contadurías, Anotadurías, or Receptorías of mortgages, or in those of the Registry of property, which have been totally or partially destroyed by fire, flood, or other casualty due to force majeure, accidental or intentional, may be restored, by again presenting the documents to which said entries referred, within the period of one year, and in accordance with the rules prescribed by this law. The Colonial Department shall, by a special order, fix the date from which said period is to be computed for each Registry.

ART. 401. In all cases the instruments shall have to be presented which contain the memorandum showing that cognizance has been taken of them, or that they have been entered or recorded in the proper book, provided that the acquisition of the estate or right is proved, before the date this law is put into operation. When the record is copied, the Register shall write and sign on the instrument another memorandum stating this fact.

ART. 402. The other documents intended to correct the inaccuracies of the recorded instruments shall also be presented.

ART. 403. The person in possession of any annuity (censo), mortgage, servitude, or any other property right in an estate, the owner of which has not recorded nor re-recorded his ownership, may request that his interest be again recorded, provided that the acquisition of the ownership or possession of the estate can be proven by the instrument or other authentic documents presented.

The record of this ownership shall be made in accordance with the general rules, and without prejudice to the right of the owner to make additions thereto, or to correct it on the presentation of new documents.

ART. 404. The owner who does not have in his possession the instruments previously recorded, and who proves the destruction or loss of the originals or of the drafts thereof, may replace this loss at any time and again record the ownership or possession, in accordance with any of the measures prescribed by Articles 390, 391, and 395.

ART. 405. Registers can not refuse to again record instruments which have already been recorded.

Should they perceive any error which can not be corrected, they shall confine themselves to showing it, so as to avoid all responsibility. Should it be capable of correction, they shall proceed in accordance with Articles 19, 66, and 402.

ART. 406. Registers who have in the books of the old offices of Contadurías, Anotadurías, or Receptorías, records corresponding to those contained in the books destroyed, shall forward a detailed statement thereof to the office where the accident happened, within the period of one year mentioned.

Without prejudice thereto, said officials shall issue true copies of the entries or records, which the interested parties may request for the purposes of this law. For these certificates they shall receive no fees.

ART. 407. When several instruments are presented which have already been recorded, showing the subsequent conveyances of the ownership of the estate, or of any of the property rights therein, they shall all be embraced in one entry.

Estates shall be given the correlative number which belongs to them, according to the order established by the Register after the destruction. In the new entries or records, there shall be stated the number which the estate has previously had.

ART. 408. The records and other entries which are replaced in accordance with this law, from the time of the destruction of the books until the determination of the period mentioned in Article 400, shall have their proper effects, with regard to the interests they set forth, according to the present laws, from the date the new entries were made.

For all legal purposes, the date of the memorandum at the foot of the instrument stating that it has been entered or recorded, shall be considered the date of the new entry. If the instruments have been lost and the date of said note or of the records referred to therein can not be proven by any other documents, the provisions of this Article shall have no effect.

ART. 409. The new entries treated of in the foregoing Article shall only pay a fifth of the usual fees mentioned in the Schedule.

ART. 410. After the period fixed in this law has elapsed, instruments which have once been recorded or entered can be again recorded, but said records or entries shall not prejudice nor favor third persons, except from their date, and the usual fees mentioned in the Schedule shall be charged therefor. Notwithstanding, the other provisions of this law are applicable to said instruments.

ART. 411. Articles 17, 20, 23, and 34, and all others referring to the effects of not recording or entering any interest, shall be suspended, with regard to estates and interests, the entries of which have disappeared, from the date of the destruction or loss of the books of the Registry until the expiration of the period allowed.

The period mentioned in this law and in the regulations for its application for the conversion of cautionary notices into definite records, shall also be suspended. The Register shall call attention to this fact and to the present Article in any certificates he may issue regarding said estates or rights. At the termination of said period, Registers must have the new indices made, or the ones existing in the respective portion of the destroyed book, must be corrected.

ART. 412. All the acts, proceedings, and documents which the persons interested may require, to make use of the privileges allowed in the present title, shall be made on stamped paper.

FINAL PROVISION.

ART. 413. All previous provisions regarding mortgages are hereby repealed. Any provisions which conflict with those of this law are also hereby repealed. None of the articles composing this law can be repealed, except by virtue of another special law, and the appropriation law can never be considered a special law for this purpose.

The periods mentioned in this law shall be computed from the time it is put into operation.

ADDITIONAL ARTICLES.

1. The Articles referring to the Royal Fees, which do not exist at present in the Philippines, as well as those referring to taxes not yet extended to said Archipelago, shall not be applied to them until opportunity offers.

By "Municipal District" (termino municipal) shall be understood in the Philippines, the one formed by the towns where there is a Captain or Petty Governor (Gobernadorcillo); by "Municipal Judge," the Justice of the Peace or Captain or Petty Governor (Gobernadorcillo), in cases where they exercise the functions of the latter; by "Municipal Public Prosecutor," where none exists, the Agricultural Supervisor (Teniente de Sementeras).

2. In Cuba and Puerto Rico, where there is no Municipal Public Prosecutor, this official shall be replaced by the Syndic of the respective Municipal Council.

3. The two foregoing provisions shall also be considered extended to all provisions of a general character, which may hereafter be enacted for the Colonies, and in which only the technical phrases used in this law shall be employed.

4. The subsidy which had been allowed Registers of Property in the Philippines by Article 313 of the Mortgage Law, which was applied to the Philippines by Royal Decree of May 10, 1889, and which is abrogated by the present one, shall continue to be enjoyed by said officials, in the same manner and during the time they are in charge of the actual Registries; all those who are not embraced in the above-mentioned case the day this law is put into operation, shall also enjoy the subsidy, but subject to any change or suppression which the Government may decree with respect to said right, in accordance with public policy and interests.

5. The fees which notaries may charge for any purpose whatsoever, in certifying to alienations, liens, or partitions, shall be the following:

For the alienation or encumbrance of any estate, the value of which does not exceed 25 pesos, 25 cents; from 25 to 75 pesos, 40 cents; from 75 to 150 pesos, 50 cents; from 150 to 250 pesos, 62 cents.

For the procedure of records relating to the partition of inheritances, when the amount involved does not exceed 1,000 pesos, 5 pesos; from 1,000 to 1,500, 7.50 pesos; from 1,500 to 2,500, 10 pesos.

The stamped paper to be employed in the records of proceedings relating to partitions, as well as in the copies thereof, shall be that bearing the seal of the last class.

6. The fees for recording sales or liens, referred to in Article 3 of this law, in its second and following paragraphs, to be charged by Registers, shall be the following:

For recording any estate or lien, the value of which does not exceed 25 pesos, 25 cents; from 25 to 75 pesos, 40 cents; from 75 to 150 pesos, 50 cents; from 150 to 250 pesos, 62 cents.

The fees to be charged by Registers for recording partitions, referred to in the same paragraphs of the Article mentioned, shall be the same as those for short records specified in Article 7 of the Schedule annexed to this law.

For recording notices referred to in Article 390, they shall charge fees in accordance with the rates established in the first paragraph of this Article.

7. Alienations referred to in the second and following paragraphs of Article 3, shall pay as tax for transfer of ownership:

For estates the value of which does not exceed 75 pesos, 50 cents per 100.

From 75 to 250 pesos, 1 per 100.

Liens created in accordance with the same Article, shall pay for estates the value of which does not exceed 75 pesos, 12 cents per 100.

From 75 to 250 pesos, 25 cents per 100.

The tax for transferring ownership of partitions or inheritances, which do not exceed 2,500 pesos, is reduced to 50 per cent of the fees fixed by this law.

8. In order that the statistical service referred to in Article 310 of this law, and of the others of the Civil Registry and Notarial Instruments placed in charge of the Registry and Notarial Division, may be made annually without difficulty, and for the purpose of defraying the expenses of printing and other necessary expenditures, the annual sum of 1,500 pesos shall be allowed in the estimates made for the Colonies. Said expenses shall be authorized by the Chief of the Registry and Notarial Division, who shall open a special item for them, of which he shall give an account, with the vouchers, to the Colonial Secretary.

9. The Presidents of the Territorial Audiencias of the Colonies, in accordance with the data which they may demand from the Judges, Delegates, and Registers of Property, and of the administrative mortgage matters they have taken part in, shall forward to the Colonial Department at the end of each year, a report stating the deficiencies and doubts they have encountered in the application of this law. They shall state therein, in detail, all questions and points of law discussed and the articles or omissions of the law which gave rise to the questions. The Colonial Secretary shall forward these reports with the report made thereon by the Registry and Notarial Division, as well as the statistics of the Registries of property, to the Committee on Codes for the Colonies. In view of this data, of the progress made in other countries, which may be utilized in our own, and of the administrative and judicial opinions in mortgage matters, the Committee on Codes shall formulate and transmit to the Government every ten years, the reforms which (in its opinion) should be introduced.

SCHEDULE OF THE FEES TO BE CHARGED BY REGISTERS OF PROPERTY.

EXAMINATIONS OF DEEDS, ENTRIES OF PRESENTATION, AND CORRESPONDING ENTRIES.

NUMBER 1.

Pesos.

For the examination, entry of presentation, marginal note and note at the foot of any instrument referring to five estates or less, the record, entry, or marginal note of which is requested, with the exception of cancellations; by instrument being understood the document or documents necessary for an entry of presentation 0. 75

NUMBER 2.

If it refers to more than five estates the following scale shall be observed:

From 6 to 10 .... 1. 00
From 11 to 20 .... 1. 50
From 21 to 30 .... 2. 00
From 31 to 50 .... 2. 50

Should it exceed this number, for the first 50, the charges shall be as specified, and for the balance, 5 centavos for each one valued at 300 pesos or more and 2 centavos for each one of a lesser value.

NUMBER 3.

When the instrument to be examined by the Register exceeds 50 folios, he shall charge for each extra folio .... .02

NUMBER 4.

If the value of the estates or rights to which the instrument refers does not reach 300 pesos, he shall charge without regard to the number of folios it may contain, or the number of estates or rights to which it refers .... .25

CANCELLATIONS.

NUMBER 5.

For all work, without regard to its form, which should be made at the instance of an interested party, for the cancellation or clearing of mortgages, annuities (censos), or property rights, including the entry of presentation and marginal notes, the following fees shall be charged for each estate:

If the estate or right is valued at less than 300 pesos........................ $2. 00
From 300 to 1,000 .... 2. 50
From 1,000 upward... 3. 75

Should the cancellation be refused or suspended, the preceding numbers of the Schedule shall be applied.

SPECIAL NOTES, RECORDS, AND ENTRIES.

NUMBER 6.

When, in consequence of the presentation no record or entry should be made but marginal notes in the old or new Registry can be made, the charge for each one shall be 50 centavos.

For each one of the notes embraced in Article 16 of the law, the same amount shall be charged.

Number 7.

For each record or entry and corresponding marginal notes, not embraced in the preceding numbers, the fixed amounts established by the following rate shall be charged:

	Records or entries in full.	Records or entries in abstract.
	Pesos.	*Pesos.*
For each estate or right which does not reach a value of 300 pesos...........	3.00	2.70
300 to 600 pesos, exclusive..	3.50	3.15
600 to 800..	4.00	3.60
800 to 1,000..	4.50	4.05
1,000 to 1,500...	5.00	4.50
1,500 to 2,000..	5.50	4.95
2,000 to 2,500..	6.00	5.40
2,500 to 3,000..	6.50	5.85
3,000 to 4,000..	7.50	6.75
4,000 to 5,000..	8.75	7.85
5,000 to 8,000..	10.00	9.00
8,000 to 10,000...	11.25	10.10
10,000 to 12,000..	12.50	11.25
12,000 to 14,000..	14.00	12.60
14,000 to 16,000..	15.50	13.95
16,000 to 18,000..	17.00	15.30
18,000 to 20,000..	18.50	16.65
20,000 to 25,000 pesos, inclusive..	20.00	18.00
Above 25,000..	25.00	22.50

For the conversion into a record of an entry made on account of an error which may be corrected, and for the suspension of entries of cautionary notices, half the fees mentioned in the preceding rates shall be charged.

COPIES OF ENTRIES, CERTIFICATES, AND SEARCH FOR DATA.

Number 8.

For copy of entries in the Registry, for each estate, without regard to its value, 50 centavos.

Number 9.

For the first page of literal certificates $1 shall be charged, irrespective of the value of the estates or rights referred to.

Number 10.

For the subsequent pages of certificates half the fees mentioned in the preceding number shall be charged.

Number 11.

For each entry regarding which a certificate in abstract is issued:
If it refers to an estate of right, the value of which is less than 300 pesos, 75 cents.
If the value thereof is 300 pesos or more, 1 peso.

Number 12.

When the certificates are to contain a reference stating that no entry at all or no entry of a specified class exists, regarding the estates or property rights, the fees shall be:
For the reference to each estate or right valued at less than 300 pesos, 35 centavos.
Of 300 pesos or over, 50 centavos.

NUMBER 13.

For the search in the old or new Registry, in order to make the statement, when the folio and book containing the record of the estate is not specified, or to issue the certificates referred to in the preceding numbers, for each estate and for each year to be searched, the fees designated in the following rate shall be charged, and in no case shall they exceed the amount fixed therein:

	For each year, if the search covers only a period of 30 years or less; and if it covers more than said period, for the first 30 years.	For each year exceeding 30 years, when the search covers 31 years or more.	Highest fee which can be charged for each estate, without regard to the number of years searched.
	Pesos.	*Pesos.*	*Pesos.*
For each estate, or right, the value of which is less than 600 pesos	0.05	0.01	3.00
600 to 1,000, exclusive	.06	.02	4.00
1,000 to 2,000	.07	.03	5.00
2,000 to 3,000	.08	.04	6.00
3,000 to 4,000	.09	.05	7.50
4,000 to 5,000	.10	.06	8.75
5,000 to 8,000	.12	.08	10.00
8,000 to 10,000	.13	.09	11.25
10,000 to 12,000	.14	.10	12.50
12,000 to 14,000	.16	.12	14.00
14,000 to 16,000	.17	.13	15.50
16,000 to 18,000	.19	.15	17.00
18,000 to 20,000	.20	.16	18.50
20,000 to 25,000, inclusive	.22	.18	20.00
25,000 and upward	.27	.23	25.00

NUMBER 14.

For the search, with regard to persons, for each person and year, irrespective of the number of estates or rights found, in the old as well as in the new Registry, the charge shall be 10 cents.

GENERAL RULES.

1. For the purpose of grading the fees, the value of an estate encumbered by a mortgage, is the price for which it was transferred, besides the value represented by the mortgages if they are in force.

2. The value of annuities (censos) and other liens of a perpetual, temporary, or redeemable character shall not be added to the price of the transfer.

3. When the transfer is made with a money consideration, the value of the estate shall be understood diminished to the extent of the amount of any liens there may be thereon.

4. With regard to the rights of use, and use and occupancy, their value shall be considered as the fourth part of the estate, and with regard to the mere ownership, three-quarters thereof.

5. For the charges of fees for leases, the amount to be paid during the entire period of the duration of the contract shall be taken as a basis. Should the period of duration of the contract not be determined, the basis shall be the amount for twelve years.

6. The fees to be charged for the registration or entry and marginal notes of servitude shall be 5 per cent of the value of the dominant estate.

7. With the object of enabling the Register to grade his fees in accordance with the provisions of this Schedule, he must take into account the contents of the instrument itself, not taking into consideration the value of encumbrances which are canceled in the Registry, should they be mentioned in the instrument. If the value of each estate or interest does not appear in the instrument, the person presenting it shall be required to state said value in a note on common paper, which shall be filed in the office. Should he not make this statement, the Register shall have a right to charge the highest fee of the proper scale or such fee as he may deem advisable.

8. When, for the purpose of ascertaining the value of some estate or property right which is transferred, it should be necessary to compute some lien thereon, affecting at the same time other property, the responsibility of each one of them not being determined, a memorandum on common paper shall be made in which all the estates subject to the lien shall be detailed, and the value of each one, so that the Register may make the proper calculation, computing the lien, with regard to the estate or interest which it is desired to enter, and the amount which, according to the value of the latter, it bears pro rata with the other encumbered estates. Should this statement not be presented, the Register need not take into consideration the encumbrance in question.

9. Registers of property must not charge any sum by way of fees without giving the person paying them a detailed receipt, who must sign his agreement therewith in the proper stub, which is to be kept in the office. Should he not be able to sign, a witness shall do so at his request.

PROVISIONAL ARTICLES.

1. The period fixed in Articles 361, 403, and corresponding ones of the mortgage law, applied to Cuba by royal decree of May 6, 1879, which is repealed by the present law, extended indefinitely by royal decree of May 6, 1882, is hereby declared as definitely closed after one year from the enactment of this law, the persons interested to whom these provisions refer, being able to enjoy the advantages allowed them therein within this period.

2. Registries in the Colonies, being reduced by this law to three classes, those of the fourth class, which are in existence in Cuba, shall hereafter be considered as of the third class. which shall be the status of their present employees from this date.

3. The Registry and Notarial Division, established by Article 265 of this law, takes the places of the Office of Civil Registers and Property and of Notaries which had been in existence, the present employees of which shall preserve all their rights in the Division, being subject to the other provisions referring to them which this law contains.

4. Notwithstanding the provisions contained in Article 1 of this law, regarding the creation, suppression, or alteration of the jurisdiction of Registries, matters which are pending shall be continued until their decision in accordance with the mortgage law previously in force in the respective Islands.

Madrid, July 14, 1893.

The Minister for the Colonies:

ANTONIO MAURA Y MONTANER.

9 7 8 3 3 3 7 3 7 8 5 2 3